A Vision Becomes Reality

Karen J. Radke, PhD, RN

and

Heather F. Fletcher, PhD, RN

TEACH Services, Inc.
P U B L I S H I N G
www.TEACHServices.com • (800) 367-1844

Copyright © 2021 Karen J. Radke and Heather F. Fletcher
Copyright © 2021 TEACH Services, Inc.
ISBN-13: 978-1-4796-1144-7 (Paperback)
ISBN-13: 978-1-4796-1145-4 (ePub)
Library of Congress Control Number: 2020906320

TEACH Services, Inc.
P U B L I S H I N G
www.TEACHServices.com • (800) 367-1844

Table of Contents

Acknowledgements

The authors are deeply grateful to the many individuals whose participation made it possible for us to conduct research and write the early history of West Indies College (now Northern Caribbean University), Andrews Memorial Hospital, and the first baccalaureate nursing programme in Jamaica. It was a major undertaking that required the expertise of each person who was willing to be involved in this project.

We would like to thank Dr. Benjamin Baker and Ashlee Chism for their expert advice on doing historical research and providing information from the Office of Archives, Statistics, and Research, General Conference of Seventh-day Adventists. We owe an enormous debt to Alton Marshalleck, former business manager/administrator at Andrews Memorial Hospital, for loaning us documents from his personal files and taking the time for multiple discussions regarding information about Andrews Memorial Hospital. We are extremely grateful to Rose Henry Morgan for sharing information about nursing at Andrews Memorial Hospital from the personal files of her mother, the late Matron Mildred Henry. We extend appreciation to Tamara Karr at Andrews University Center for Adventist Research for providing information about Andrews Memorial Hospital from the Muriel E. Chapman Collection.

We regret that Rebecca Gucilatar-Jakobsen, first chairman of West Indies College Department of Nursing Education, passed away several years ago before we started this project. We are forever indebted to her for the sterling contribution she made by writing a report at the end of her five years of outstanding leadership regarding early development of the department and implementation of the baccalaureate nursing programme. Moreover, we are forever indebted to the late Lois Dujon, the late Laurice Hunter-Scott, the late Enid Lawrence, the late Gertrude Swaby, and the late Norma Woodham for their ongoing support as West Indies College developed the Department of Nursing Education and the baccalaureate nursing programme.

We value the contribution of Seth Bates at Loma Linda University Heritage Research Center for information about Seventh-day Adventist nurse leaders. We also recognize the late Honourable Syringa Marshall-Burnett and Hilda M. Ming for information about nurse leaders and nursing education in Jamaica.

We are profoundly grateful to West Indies College nurse graduates Christine Barnes, Maggie Burrows-Turner, Marilyn Clare-Moreau, Dr. Joan Collins-Ricketts, Evadne Cox-McCleary, Leonarda Dowdie-McKenzie, Ilene (Irene) Gentles-Patrick, Dr. Judith Clayton Gomez, Audrey Grant-Lewin, Doreen Hardware, Elaine Haughton, Sonia Kennedy-Brown, Shirlene McLean-Henriques, Beverley McPherson, Rose

Henry Morgan, Maxine Smith-Webley, and Beverley Tai-Binger for recalling and/ or verifying information about the Andrews Memorial Hospital campus and their baccalaureate nursing programme, sharing about their lives beyond graduation, providing photographs, and even loaning us their yearbooks. We also thank them for their encouragement to complete this historical work and have it published. We were reminded, "Don't let it sit on the shelf," and "God has a job for you to finish so no laying down on the job yet."

A special word of gratitude goes to Marilyn Badzik, Elena Burke-Thomas, Dr. Ronald Hartman, Dr. Patricia S. Jones, Myrtle Nelson Morgan, Kenneth Morris, Valerie Nusantara, Anita Pearson Schultz, and Dr. Ouida E. Spleen Westney for information about Andrews Memorial Hospital as well as to Terry and Rhonda Griswold for recalling information about the women's dormitory on the Andrews Memorial Hospital campus. We also thank Dr. Edna Ashmeade, Dr. Gloria Barnes-Gregory, the late Shirley Gallimore, Arlene Kim Greer, Glee Hartman, and Jo Ann Jones for recalling information about the baccalaureate nursing programme.

We applaud the excellent service provided by the library staff at the Hiram S. Walters Resource Centre, Northern Caribbean University, for locating information on the early history of West Indies College: Andrew Gooden, Tannique Muir, Nicola Palmer, Hortense Riley, and especially Shannette Smith, who did a stellar job, time and again. We also express our gratitude to Beverly Henry for information on the early history of West Indies College, Susan Long Gordon for information about the beginning of the alumni organization, and Dr. Aston Barnes for information on the process used to approve a new academic programme.

We appreciate Jennifer Bartley, who verified courses taken at West Indies College, and Joyce Malcolm, who verified names of West Indies College graduates and dates of graduation. We also appreciate the technical support provided by the Northern Caribbean University Department of Nursing staff: Erica Fearon, Una Morris, and Dion Thompson, administrative assistants; Yvonne Taffe, secretary; and Shamar Francis, student worker.

We recognize and thank Howard and Doreen English, Lee Herbert Fletcher III, Olive Fletcher, Vivian Geow, Dr. Newton Hoilette, Dr. Yvette Holness, Kresten Jakobsen, David Klingbeil, Jonathan Klingbeil, Rilla Klingbeil, Alton Marshalleck, Rose Henry Morgan, Leticia Russell, Cheryl Standish, Ath Tuot, Marlo J. Waters, and Dr. Charles Wilkens for biographical information; Ashlee Chism, the late Astley Fletcher, Evelyn Hitchcock, Paul Kluczynski, and Wilmer Radke for technical assistance with photographs; and June Kimball Strong, prolific author, for her critique of the manuscript and valuable suggestions.

We are most grateful to Dr. Lincoln Edwards, president, and I. E. 'Yvonne' Bignall, vice-president for university relations, at Northern Caribbean University, as well as Dr. Marvin Rouhotas, president/chief executive officer, and Keith Shakespeare, vice-president of operations, at Andrews Memorial Hospital for their support and for permission to use archived documents and photographs. We also thank other individuals who gave permission to use selected information and/or photographs: Carol Bent-Wright, Nadine Buckland, Jim Ford, Pastor Mamerto Guingguing, Linette

Mitchell, Ron Nelson, Briana Pastorino, Tim Poirier, Pastor-Dr. Leonard Steele, Vincent Sullivan, Brigadier General (Retired) Loree K. Sutton, MD, and Shanalee Tamares.

The authors greatly appreciate the knowledge, guidance, and support made readily available to them by the publishing team at TEACH Services, Inc. It was a pleasure and a privilege to work with such outstanding individuals who assisted us in bringing this project to completion: Bill Newman, publisher, design and layout; Timothy Hullquist, author advisor; Rebecca Silver, editing; Mariana Salter, product development; Alyssa Newman, production; and Alison Lopez-Ramirez, marketing.

Preface

This is the story of how a Seventh-day Adventist educational institution, West Indies College (now Northern Caribbean University) in Mandeville, Jamaica, collaborated with a Seventh-day Adventist health care institution, Andrews Memorial Hospital in Kingston, Jamaica, to develop and implement the Department of Nursing Education and the first baccalaureate nursing programme in Jamaica. It was of paramount importance to the Seventh-day Adventist church leaders in Jamaica and the West Indies region along with administrative personnel at Andrews Memorial Hospital that professional nurses be prepared with a Christ-centred collegiate education to care for the spiritual needs of patients as well as their physical and emotional needs.

The early history of this endeavour has never been published. In 2009, Heather Fletcher, who was a faculty member in the Department of Nursing at Northern Caribbean University, began to gather historical information in the oral tradition characteristic of the Jamaican culture. Five years later through the providence of God, Dr. Fletcher met Dr. Radke who was acting chairman of the baccalaureate nursing programme in the third year (1972–1973) of its implementation. Both of us are alumna of Loma Linda University School of Nursing in California and through that avenue became acquainted. It soon became apparent that we were eager to do the necessary research regarding how the baccalaureate nursing programme began and to preserve its history in written form.

Although this task was formidable and filled with uncertainty, each step also proved to be filled with wholehearted anticipation of what we would learn next. One of the most daunting aspects of this adventure was to find historical information and then be certain of its accuracy. We learned the importance of complete and accurate documentation and to archive both documents and photographs in an organized manner for others to use. We also learned that knowing the past history of an institution can be inspiring and insightful. It can make one wiser in the decisions to be made and the path to be taken.

Many individuals employed at Northern Caribbean University readily provided information as did those at the Office of Archives, Statistics, and Research, General Conference of Seventh-day Adventists. However, locating key individuals who were involved in the college, hospital, and baccalaureate nursing programme almost fifty years later was a challenge. It was time consuming but well worth the effort. We learned that people were more than willing to share documents they saved and information they recalled. On the other hand, our search led us to be painfully aware that some had passed away. However, we were blessed to have the privilege of listening to their family members share cherished memories with us.

The story begins with a narrative about Pastor Hiram Sebastian Walters, who was president of the West Indies Union Conference. He was the Seventh-day Adventist church leader who envisioned West Indies College offering a baccalaureate nursing programme in affiliation with Andrews Memorial Hospital. The first chapter also includes an overview of the trends in nursing education that were occurring at the time in the Caribbean region. The next chapter is about the early history of West Indies College (1907–1969) followed by the early history of Andrews Memorial Hospital (1944–1969). The philosophy, mission, and values of each institution are presented because of the impact they had on designing the baccalaureate nursing curriculum. Subsequent chapters focus on the planning, development, implementation, and progression of the programme from 1969 to 1976, that includes additional history about the college and the hospital during those years. The story climaxes with how some of the early graduates went forth to serve God and humanity. An epilogue is included to share with the readers how God has abundantly blessed Northern Caribbean University Department of Nursing for almost fifty years.

It is our hope that the content will provide information on the early history of Seventh-day Adventist higher education and medical work in Jamaica as well as provide a blueprint of the process used in developing what is now Northern Caribbean University Department of Nursing and its baccalaureate nursing programme. We share the issues encountered, how challenges were met, the goals to be achieved, and highlights of the Department of Nursing as it approaches its fiftieth anniversary in 2020.

—Karen J. Radke (New York, USA) and Heather F. Fletcher (Mandeville, Jamaica)

CHAPTER 1

A Fearless Visionary

Hiram S. Walters
President
West Indies Union Conference of Seventh-day Adventists
1968 to 1976
Photo: Courtesy of Northern Caribbean University.

Hiram Sebastian Walters was the man who envisioned that someday West Indies College (WIC, now Northern Caribbean University) in Mandeville, Jamaica, would have a Department of Nursing Education that would offer a baccalaureate nursing programme in association with Andrews Memorial Hospital (AMH) in Kingston, Jamaica.[1] Both of these institutions are operated by the Seventh-day Adventist Church.

Walters "was born July 15, 1917, in La Boca, Canal Zone, Panama, to Jamaican parents, James Samuel and Amy Morgan Walters." His mother, a Seventh-day Adventist Bible Worker, "prayed often that her only son, affectionately known as 'Tim,' would grow up to be a preacher, so she 'trained him for God from his early youth.'"[2]

In 1940, Walters graduated from the ministerial course at West Indian Training College, Mandeville, Jamaica. He was known to be "a tireless conversationalist, friend, and confidante." In 1942, he married his special friend, Anna Lucille Jones from Darliston, Westmoreland Parish, Jamaica. Pastor and Mrs. Walters then migrated to the United States for a few years. He immediately conducted a successful evangelistic crusade in Nyack, New York.[3] Subsequently, he earned a bachelor's degree in theology from Oakwood College, Huntsville, Alabama, in 1948.[4] Although Pastor Walters had the opportunity for permanent employment in the United States, he insisted on returning to Jamaica.[5]

In the mid-1960s, Walters was interviewed by Arthur E. Sutton from Loma Linda, California. At the time, Pastor Walters was president of the Central Jamaica Conference of Seventh-day Adventists.[6] Sutton's mission was to gather information first hand regarding the educational and medical programmes of the Seventh-day Adventist Church in Jamaica.[7] In his book, *Jamaica: Island of Miracles*, Sutton describes Walters as a tall, powerful man with a personality that commanded respect and one who forcefully expressed his views. Referring to the work of the church, Walters told Sutton, "I face the future with confidence. You've got to have confidence, you know, or you don't have leadership."[8] He continued by saying, "We must have vision. We cannot be timid. We must break with old methods, worn-out ways of doing things."[9] He concluded his comments with the words, "God cannot use fearful people. If you are fearful, you are useless. These are days for courage."[10]

Pastor Walters began to articulate his vision of a baccalaureate nursing programme in 1968[11] when he was elected president of the West Indies Union Conference of Seventh-day Adventists.[12] He was also chairman of the Board of Trustees at WIC[13] and chairman of the Board of Directors at AMH.[14] Thus, he was in a position to spearhead discussions about a baccalaureate nursing programme among the church leaders as well as among decision makers at the college and the hospital. The discussions were timely because it was of paramount importance to the Seventh-day Adventist church leaders in Jamaica and the West Indies region along with administrative personnel at AMH that professional nurses be prepared with a Christ-centred collegiate education to care for the spiritual needs of patients as well as their physical and emotional needs.[15]

In 1968, there were only two schools of nursing in Jamaica that prepared general nurses— Kingston School of Nursing, which was the Teaching Department at Kingston Public Hospital, and University College Hospital (later University Hospital of the West Indies) School of Nursing, Mona. Both of these hospitals provided a three-year, diploma nursing programme. However, a different model of education was needed that would advance the status of registered general nurses in Jamaica and the West Indies. Gertrude Hildegard Swaby, one of the trailblazers in nursing education,[16] was adamant that hospital programmes preparing general nurses be incorporated within tertiary educational institutions.[17]

For several years, Seventh-day Adventist colleges and universities had offered a four-year, baccalaureate nursing programme in other parts of the world. Thus, "Walters was determined that WIC would offer a similar nursing programme in affiliation with AMH."[18] It would be the first tertiary-based nursing programme in

Jamaica. Being an energetic and inspirational leader, it would take only a short period of time for his vision to become a reality.

Pastor Walters was a fearless warrior and a man of undeniable courage in pursuing goal after goal that benefited the Seventh-day Adventist Church and the people of Jamaica. After giving thirty-five years of dedicated service, he retired in 1976.[19]

Needless to say, Hiram S. Walters was most deserving of the honours he received in his lifetime. In October 1970, the government of Jamaica awarded him the Order of Distinction. For the first time in Jamaica's history, special recognition was given to over seventy citizens of the country for civic and religious achievements.[20]

In April 1990, the Central Jamaica Conference officially opened the H. S. Walters Clinic (now the H. S. Walters Health Care Centre) in Sydenham, Spanish Town, Jamaica. This was done "in honor of a stalwart, visionary pioneer."[21]

On June 7, 1992, Northern Caribbean University held an opening ceremony for the new library. It was named the Hiram S. Walters Resource Centre "after one of Adventism's greatest champions in the Caribbean."[22]

On August 4, 2001, Northern Caribbean University conferred on Pastor Walters the honorary degree, doctor of divinity.[23] In a tribute to Dr. Walters titled, "Humility of a Giant," he was described as "Seventh-day Adventism personified in Jamaica." It was also noted that "his influence had a worldwide ripple effect on the global Seventh-day Adventist community."[24]

After living a life devoted to the cause of God, Hiram Sebastian Walters died on October 2, 2001.[25] He left a rich legacy that resulted from his dynamic and steadfast leadership for the Seventh-day Adventist denomination.

CHAPTER 2

West Indies College — A Light on the Hill

The gospel message as proclaimed by the Seventh-day Adventist Church spread rapidly throughout Jamaica[1] after Pastor A. J. Haysmer of Michigan and his wife were appointed missionaries to this Caribbean Island in 1893.[2] Ten years later,[3] there were 1,188 Sabbath-keeping members and seventeen churches in Jamaica[4] due to the labours of different workers.[5] The time had come to form "a more central organization" as the work continued to flourish.[6] Thus, in 1903, the Jamaica Conference of Seventh-day Adventists was organized[7] with J. B. Beckner as its first president.[8] At the organizational meeting, W. A. Spicer, secretary of the General Conference of Seventh-day Adventists,[9] commented, "As the work grows in Jamaica, I believe it will be able in due time to furnish us faithful and disciplined labourers for other fields. A training school is greatly desired by all."[10]

West Indies College (now Northern Caribbean University) began as that "greatly desired" training school[11] to prepare gospel workers[12] for the West Indies, tropical Africa, and the southern states in North America.[13] It was a training school that combined intellectual and spiritual development of its students with a practical education.[14]

In 1906, the Jamaica Conference of Seventh-day Adventists, under the leadership of President Beckner,[15] secured monetary pledges and cash from the Jamaican Adventist believers towards establishing the training school.[16,17] On May 10, 1906, sixty-six acres of land was purchased from Elias Levy Stannigar of Linstead and the title registered in the names of Judson Barkley Beckner, Jannus Addison Strickland, and Wellington Frederick Burkley,[18] members of the Jamaica Conference Executive Committee.[19] The land was about twenty-five miles from Kingston, and a mile and a half from the Bog Walk railway station. Additionally, forty-one acres adjoining this property was acquired as a lease and sale arrangement. They took possession of the land on June 10, 1906.[20] The site for the school building, farm, and pasture at Willowdene, St. Catherine Parish,[21] was described as "beautiful and the scenery magnificent."[22] It soon became evident, however, that in spite of faithful giving by the Jamaican believers, the financial means were not sufficient to support a school without the help of the entire West Indian field. On June 26, 1906, the West Indian Union Conference of Seventh-day Adventists was organized with headquarters in Kingston, Jamaica,[23] and with George F. Enoch as president.[24] "It was decided finally that the entire West Indian

Field would co-operate for the establishment of this school and that it would be a Union Conference Institution."[25]

Once again, however, the financial resources were not sufficient for such an endeavour that would cost at least US $10,000.[26] Therefore, the West Indian Union Conference petitioned the General Conference of Seventh-day Adventists Executive Committee to assist in establishing the school.[27] On July 24, 1906, the General Conference Executive Committee voted that Enoch could solicit funds in the United States and that the General Conference would donate to the West Indian field 2,000 copies of the book, *Christ's Object Lessons,* by Ellen G. White, to be sold and the money used to help secure the school.[28] Then on October 10, 1906, the General Conference Executive Committee voted to donate another 1,000 copies of *Christ's Object Lessons* provided the books were sold by July 1, 1907.[29] In addition, the General Conference appropriated US $5,000 for the school.[30]

In January 1907,[31] Professor C. B. Hughes and his wife, Ella,[32] of Texas[33] arrived in Jamaica.[34] Shortly thereafter in March,[35] West Indian Training School was opened[36] with the eight boys enrolled who helped President Beckner prepare the ground at Willowdene.[37] The school would eventually develop into West Indies College and then become Northern Caribbean University.

> *"It was decided finally that the entire West Indian Field would co-operate for the establishment of this school and that it would be a Union Conference Institution."*

C. B. Hughes, wife Ella, and child. Hughes was the first principal of West Indian Training School. Photo: Courtesy of the Ellen G. White Estate.

The school and home at Willowdene had an assembly room and a room for the boys on the first floor. There were four rooms and a veranda for dining on the second floor.[38] Professor Hughes was the principal, business manager, and teacher (Bible and history). Ella Hughes served on the West Indian Training School Managing Board.[39] Then in May 1907,[40] E. C. Cushman and his wife, Mary,[41] of Nebraska[42] arrived in Jamaica. Mr. Cushman's responsibility was to oversee and direct the students in their work outdoors.[43] He also taught a course (mathematics) as did Mary Cushman (physiology and simple treatments). Other classes were taught by H. H. Cobban (bookkeeping), and Mrs. Nannie E. Bender (organ). It is unknown as to who taught English.[44]

West Indian Training School-Home.

Prior to the Cushmans' arrival, however, the "West Indian Union workers discovered the land [Willowdene] was unsuitable for a successful farm."[45] This meant that the site would not be successful as an industrial training school, and the property was sold.[46] With additional financial assistance from the General Conference,[47] 507 acres of land was purchased in Riversdale, St. Catherine Parish, about six miles north of Willowdene and a mile-and-a-half from the Riversdale railway station. The property had been part of a large sugar estate. Different tropical fruit trees, cacao trees, and banana plants were abundant. The land was suitable for growing vegetable crops and for cattle to graze. There also were woods on the property from which timber could be obtained to erect more buildings. On September 2, 1907, the faculty and students began moving to the Riversdale location.[48]

By June 1909, there were thirty-six students—twenty-seven young men and nine young women. Only a few young ladies were admitted because there was no employment for them except housework. Most of the students were from Jamaica, but some were from Barbados, Dominica, Haiti, Panama, and Trinidad. There were five faculty: C. B. Hughes, E. C. Cushman, Mary Cushman, E. C. Wood, and his wife, Pearl.[49,50]

Unfortunately, after offering high school lessons and vocational classes for about six years, the school was temporarily closed in 1913 due to the declining health of teachers and students, and ongoing financial issues.[51] According to the testimonial of Lee Fletcher as told to Beverly Henry on November 17, 1976, "malaria was the main cause of illness." Lee Fletcher was the son of Pastor Hubert Fletcher, who was one of the early, Jamaican, Seventh-day Adventist ministers. Lee Fletcher was also the father of L. Herbert Fletcher, who was president of West Indies College at the time of the interview.[52] The land was sold except for thirteen acres.[53]

In 1918, G. A. Roberts, president of the Jamaica Conference of Seventh-day Adventists,[54] heard about a 171-acre piece of property that was called Cedar Grove and owned by Edwin Charley of Kingston.[55] The property, located two miles south of Mandeville, was purchased on which to rebuild the West Indian Training School.[56] Situated on a hilltop at an elevation of more than 2,000 feet above sea level in the mountainous region of Manchester Parish,[57] the property was renamed Coolsworthy.[58]

G. A. Roberts, president of the Jamaica Conference.
Photo: Courtesy of Northern Caribbean University.

On April 15, 1918, President Roberts presented to the General Conference Executive Committee a budget of US $8,449.00 for the school. The Executive Committee voted to allocate the necessary funds "with the understanding that in the future the Mission Board pay only for the teachers of the school, leaving other expenses to be met from the tuition or funds raised within the union."[59]

President Roberts, C. B. Hughes, and his wife Ella, who returned to Jamaica,[60] and Johanna Daw of California[61] were instrumental in restarting the school.[62] On January 6, 1919, school was opened with the first group of students in a rented house on Caledonia Road in Mandeville.[63] Hughes was once again the principal [64] and taught courses as did his wife Ella and Miss Daw.[65] In the meantime, buildings from the Riversdale property were dismantled and transported to the Coolsworthy property to be reassembled.[66] In August 1919, the school continued its operation on the Coolsworthy property.[67]

The following month,[68] W. H. Wineland and his wife, both from Illinois,[69] joined the teaching staff.[70] In 1920, Hughes, who spent part of his time on the farm, unfortunately sustained injuries while using a plough and was forced to retire. Subsequently, Wineland became the principal.[71] In June 1923, the first class of three students graduated from the twelfth grade.[72]

Johanna Daw, a teacher at West Indian Training School.
Photo: Courtesy of Northern Caribbean University.

In 1924, the school expanded to fourteen grades and was now a junior college.[73] The name, therefore, was changed from West Indian Training School to West Indian Training College.[74] Organizationally, the college included the elementary (normal practice) school with grades one to eight, the secondary school (high school) with grades nine to twelve, and the advanced educational level (junior college) with grades thirteen and fourteen. Three curricula were offered at the advanced educational level: the Ministerial Course, the Normal Course to prepare primary school teachers, and the Commercial Course.[75]

In 1926, the first class of four students received their diplomas and graduated from the junior college.[76] Later that year, the Old Students and Teachers' Association was formed with the purpose of fostering a spirit of "unity and good fellowship" as well as a "spirit of loyalty and devotion" to their alma mater. Mr. P. J. Bailey was the association's first president.[77] The official organ of the association was *The Witconian*.[78] "This was the genesis of an informal alumni association."[79]

After giving almost eight years of dedicated service in Jamaica, Wineland and his family went on furlough in 1927.[80] For the next fifty-three years the college continued to grow under the leadership of Presidents F. O. Rathbun, O. W. Tucker, R. E. Shafer, H. D. Isaacs, R. S. J. Hamilton, F. S. Thompson, M. J. Sorensen, C. L. von Pohle, B. G. Butherus, M. J. Sorensen (served a second time as president), W. A. Sowers, Leif Kr. Tobiassen, W. A. Osborne, Sydney O. Beaumont (the first Jamaican president), K. G. Vaz, C. D. Standish, and L. H. Fletcher.[81]

Many young people sought an education at West Indian Training College, although some of them were not Seventh-day Adventists or even Christians.[82] By 1936, students from Antigua, Bermuda, British Honduras, Costa Rica, Cuba, Guatemala,

Jamaica, Nicaragua, Panama, Peru, Spain, Trinidad, and the United States were enrolled at West Indian Training College.[83,84,85]

West Indian Training College.
Photo: Courtesy of Northern Caribbean University.

From the beginning in 1907, the faculty committed to developing the head, the hand, and the heart—the mental, physical, and spiritual dimensions—of its students.[86] Thus, in addition to educating the mind, the college implemented a work-study programme and established several industries such as the farm (crops and livestock), dairying, tailoring, furniture factory, cabinet making, sheet metal factory, plumbing, bakery, and printery.[87,88,89,90] These industries provided valuable training for the students as well as employment to help them defray the costs of tuition and board.[91] The laundry, kitchen, and campus maintenance provided other opportunities for training and employment.[92] A cannery and cement block factory were added later.[93]

This Seventh-day Adventist Christian college on the hill placed special emphasis on developing the heart—the spiritual aspect—of its students. Bible classes were a required part of the curriculum for every student.[94] Morning and evening worship[95] were held in Jamaica Hall, the ladies' dormitory, and in Cedar Hall, the men's dormitory.[96] During the week, daily chapel was held in the auditorium for faculty and students.[97] "Some presentations were inspirational and others broadened the scope of general knowledge."[98] Friday evening vespers were held to usher in the Sabbath day that began at sunset and continued until sunset on Saturday night.[99] There was also a Week of Prayer held both in the fall[100] and in the spring.[101] It was a time when students renewed their consecration to God while others gave their hearts to the Lord and later were baptized.[102]

> *From the beginning in 1907, the faculty committed to developing the head, the hand, and the heart—the mental, physical, and spiritual dimensions—of its students.*

The students were encouraged to participate in various facets of the church's work, such as providing leadership in Sabbath School,[103] which was a time to discuss various Scriptures, and participating in church services held on Saturday. All students had the opportunity to learn how to give sermons, Bible studies, and inspirational talks.[104] Many students—men and women—worked as colporteurs during the summer months selling books and magazine subscriptions published by the Seventh-day Adventist denomination to earn a portion of their college expenses.[105]

The faculty were also committed to addressing the social needs and developing the social skills of the students. As early as the 1920s, the Excelsior Club for men and the Philmelodia Club for women were formed. In addition to developing social skills, the young men and women developed leadership skills by conducting worship services in their respective dormitories, did fundraising projects, and provided community service.[106] Then in February 1936, the United Student Movement was organized. One major purpose of this organization was for students to have more opportunities for mutual participation in college life with the administration and faculty. Some of the organization's goals were to encourage loyalty to the school and its Christian values,… promote spiritual activities on campus,…support student campaigns that would develop leadership skills, and form a committee on social affairs that would provide for proper cultural training.[107]

Five months later, the United Student Movement began publishing a school paper, *The College Echo*, to advertise information about the college and spread the college interests to a community that went far beyond the borders of its campus—all of Jamaica and the large Seventh-day Adventist constituency in the Inter-American region.[108] The college press printed the first issue of *The College Echo* on July 15, 1936.[109] Eventually, the students produced a college yearbook. Various names of the yearbook were *The College Echo*, *Witconian*, and *Hilltop Echo*.[110] Since 1960, the yearbook has been named *Palm Leaves* "in honour of the beautiful, stately royal palms" on campus.[111]

As with any institution, renovation and improvement of buildings as well as constructing new buildings were constant projects. In 1930, the library was renovated while the dormitories and dining room were improved.[112] Unfortunately, on October 24, 1935, a raging fire occurred in the engine room and dynamo room of the Wood Products Department that resulted in the loss of both rooms and damage to the equipment. However, the rest of the wood products building was saved due to the heroic efforts of the young men and women who formed a bucket brigade of water to douse the flames. Repairs and rebuilding began, and the college moved forward.[113]

In 1946, a new building for the Wood Products Department was completed, and its former building was remodelled to house the college press. The old printery was transformed into a beautiful dining room.[114] It was also necessary to erect a model church school building to facilitate effective teaching of the children in the Mandeville Seventh-day Adventist Church.[115]

By 1951, it was essential to initiate a five-year rebuilding programme at West Indian Training College.[116] The original, wooden buildings had been eaten by termites and were rapidly deteriorating. Repairing or remodelling them was impossible.[117] Furthermore, with a rapid, yearly increase in enrolment,[118] the students were crowded in the dormitories and classrooms.[119] The time had come "to meet a "long-felt need of expanding our college facilities."[120]

Funds were necessary for this endeavour to be successful. Pastor Joe Fletcher, secretary of the Missionary Volunteer and Educational Departments of the West Jamaica Conference of Seventh-day Adventists, issued a clarion call to all within the British West Indies Union Mission, "Let us Arise, Give, Gather, and Build for God and our youth."[121] It was a timely appeal because on the night of August 17, 1951,[122] Hurricane Charlie swept through Jamaica, damaging most of the buildings on the college campus and destroying many trees. Fortunately, no one was injured. In a short amount of time, the buildings were repaired and able to be used, and the college was once again forging ahead.[123]

In 1953, a new administration building that included offices, a chapel, library, and classrooms was built.[124] Over the next four years, a recreation centre was completed,[125] a new print shop was erected,[126] and the new girls' dormitory was built.[127] Eventually, a new cafeteria and dining room were completed.[128]

During the years of rebuilding, the faculty expanded its advanced educational offerings. As of 1946, two years of college training could also be obtained in the Bible Workers Course, Music Course, and Secretarial Course.[129] Then in 1956, West Indian Training College offered a four-year ministerial programme leading to the bachelor of theology degree.[130] Three years later, senior college status was granted to the Department of Theology.[131] Thus, West Indian Training College was renamed West Indies College, in 1959.[132]

Entrance to West Indies College administration building (near right) in 1973.
It also housed the chapel and library. Cedar Hall (men's dormitory, far right).
The roof of the music building can be seen in between.
Photo by Karen J. Radke.

On July 7, 1960, the General Conference Executive Committee authorized West Indies College to offer another four-year college programme leading to the bachelor of education degree for teaching at the secondary level.[133] Principal and subsidiary teaching fields known as major and minor areas of interest were initiated: business administration, English, history, music, natural sciences, religion, secretarial sciences, and social sciences.[134]

West Indies College Department of Teacher Education building (near left) in 1973.
Jamaica Hall (women's dormitory, in the middle). Sorensen Hall (cafeteria and classrooms, near right).
Photo by Karen J. Radke.

By 1967, intense efforts were being made to upgrade the quality of instruction and academic standards, not only in Jamaica, but throughout the Inter-American Division of Seventh-day Adventists. Faculty were attending in-service training sessions, national universities, and institutions of higher learning outside of their own countries.[135]

As of 1969, West Indies College had graduated more than 1,000 students from the college division.[136] In the same year, West Indies College offered a four-year programme leading to the degree, bachelor of science in business administration.[137] Moreover, in 1969, Kenneth G. Vaz, MA, who was a Jamaican national and in his final year as president of West Indies College, did some preliminary legwork regarding a four-year, baccalaureate nursing programme.[138] The college continued to provide diploma programmes at the junior college level in arts and science, business administration, primary teacher education, and secretarial science as well as a five-year course leading to the Cambridge General Certificate of Education Examination that qualified one for admission to a college or university.[139]

Through the years West Indies College and its environment were described as "a haven where nature and revelation unite in education."[140] The college on the hill overlooked luxuriant, green vegetation characteristic of a tropical climate in the tranquil countryside of Mandeville. The buildings on campus were enhanced, not only with the beauty of stately royal palm trees, but also with flamboyant royal poinciana trees, pine trees, and an array of colourful bougainvillea and hibiscus.[141]

Kenneth G. Vaz, president of West Indies College, 1964–1970.
Photo: Courtesy of Northern Caribbean University.

From West Indies College, a commanding view of luxuriant, green vegetation;
the West Indies College aeroplane strip; Shooters Hill to the left; and
the Blue Mountain range in the far distance just right of Shooters Hill in 1973.
Photo by Karen J. Radke. Caption by Beverly Henry and Karen J. Radke.

A view of West Indies College on the hill in 1973.
Photo by Karen J. Radke.

> *Through the years West Indies College and its environment were described as "a haven where nature and revelation unite in education."*

It was a college preparing young people to go forth to carry the gospel of Jesus Christ through the ministry of their chosen profession. By the grace of God and with fervent prayers ascending, West Indies College would continue to grow and be a light on the hill to glorify God.

CHAPTER 3

Andrews Memorial Hospital— Healing and Teaching

Health ministries, such as providing health care and teaching principles of healthful living, have been a long-established mission of the Seventh-day Adventist Church, penetrating the farthest outreaches around the world. The year was 1943. Officers of the General Conference of Seventh-day Adventists and of the Inter-American Division of Seventh-day Adventists recognized an urgent need for the church to begin medical work in Jamaica.[1] The following year, the British West Indies Union Mission was organized with Pastor Robert H. Pierson as superintendent.[2] Under his leadership, plans were made to have a hospital, a clinic, and a school of nursing.[3]

In March 1944, Sulgrave Manor, a large residence on Hope Road near King's House in the beautiful Kingston suburb of Half Way Tree, was purchased.[4] In due time, Sulgrave Manor would be renovated and renamed J. N. Andrews Memorial Hospital (AMH)[5] in honour of John Nevins Andrews,[6] who was the first Seventh-day Adventist pioneer missionary to go from the United States to Europe in 1874.[7]

Dr. Clifford Russell Anderson. The first medical director of Andrews Memorial Hospital.
Photo: Andrews Memorial Hospital Photograph Album, AMHPA-I-02-1, Department of Archives and Special Collections, Loma Linda University, Loma Linda, California.

Ruth M. Munroe. The first matron of Andrews Memorial Hospital and director of Andrews Memorial Hospital School of Nursing.
Photo: Courtesy of Linette Mitchell from her book, Thy Light Is Come: A Short History of the Seventh-day Adventist Church in Jamaica (Mandeville, Jamaica, W. I.: West Indies College Press, 1990), 39.

Towards the end of 1944, Dr. Clifford R. Anderson of Washington, D.C.,[8] and Ruth M. Munroe, BSNE, RN (bachelor of science in nursing education, registered nurse), who had recently earned her degree at Washington Missionary College (now Washington Adventist University) in Takoma Park, Maryland,[9] arrived in Jamaica.[10] Munroe had previous administrative experience as a missionary nurse in Japan, the Philippines, and Thailand.[11] Anderson and Munroe immediately began the task of developing and organizing AMH, the first Seventh-day Adventist hospital in the Inter-American Division.[12]

In the meantime, faithful Adventist believers of the North Street Seventh-day Adventist Church in downtown Kingston, Jamaica, raised the necessary funds so that the leadership could secure land behind the church.[13] The property, located at 56 James Street,[14] was then turned over to the AMH Board of Directors to erect a clinic that would provide health services to the less privileged people of Jamaica.[15]

After spending a few months back in the United States, Dr. Anderson returned to Jamaica with his family in the early part of 1945. He had accepted the call to be medical director at AMH, which included the clinic on James Street. Anderson was also appointed medical secretary of the Inter-American Division and the British West Indies Union Mission. Shortly thereafter, Robert E. Gibson, who was working in the Chesapeake Conference (Maryland), and his family arrived in Kingston.[16] Gibson assumed his responsibilities as business manager and general administrator of the hospital to continue establishing and organizing the Seventh-day Adventist denomination's first major medical work in the Caribbean.[17] Ruth Munroe was appointed the hospital matron (director of nursing service) and director of the hospital's school of nursing.[18]

Robert E. Gibson and Family. Gibson was the first business manager and general administrator of Andrews Memorial Hospital.
Photo: Andrews Memorial Hospital Photograph Album, AMHPA-I-51-1, Department of Archives and Special Collections, Loma Linda University, Loma Linda, California.

On December 12, 1945, Andrews Memorial Clinic on James Street was opened to the public by the Honourable H. M. Foot, Acting Governor of Jamaica, Office of the British Empire. His Excellency said, "I think to any individual or to any organization

Andrews Memorial Clinic at 56 James Street, Kingston.
Photo: Andrews Memorial Hospital Photograph Album, AMHPA-I-93-1, Department of Archives and Special Collections, Loma Linda University, Loma Linda, California.

which is engaged in public or social work we can wisely apply the old Biblical test: 'By their fruits ye shall know them!' This afternoon we are seeing the fruits of the efforts of this community to make their contribution to a better Kingston ... This is indeed a very remarkable contribution by a comparatively small community."[19]

The clinic had an operating theatre, X-ray and laboratory facilities, a medicine dispensary, and treatment rooms.[20] The front part of the clinic was used to provide out-patient services and had office space for physicians to consult with the patients. The back area of the clinic was used for in-patients.[21] The clinic had about twenty beds. Charges were reduced for those who had limited funds, and health care was free to those who could not afford to pay anything.[22]

Throughout 1945 and much of 1946, work continued to transform Sulgrave Manor into AMH. Ruth Munroe's father, Clarence Munroe, supervised the workmen who were engaged in remodelling and redecorating the manor. Treatment rooms were

East end of Sulgrave Manor, which faced north, transformed into the east section of the original Andrews Memorial Hospital.
Photo: Andrews Memorial Hospital Photograph Album, AMHPA-I-04-2, Department of Archives and Special Collections, Loma Linda University, Loma Linda, California.

West end of Sulgrave Manor, which faced north, transformed into the west section of the original Andrews Memorial Hospital.
Photo: Andrews Memorial Hospital Photograph Album, AMHPA-I-04-3, Department of Archives and Special Collections, Loma Linda University, Loma Linda, California.

reconstructed for electrotherapy, hydrotherapy, and massage. Equipment, supplies, and furnishings were obtained for departments of the hospital as well as furnishings for the patients' rooms. Clarence Munroe also served as physiotherapist and dietician.[23]

By August 1946, the hospital on Hope Road was running smoothly and efficiently.[24] Pastor D. V. Pond, superintendent of the East Jamaica Mission, and Pastor D. B. Reid, a member of the executive committee,[25] were instrumental in working out the details of erecting a clinic building and transforming Sulgrave Manor into AMH.[26] The General Conference of Seventh-day Adventists and the Inter-American Division gave generously of their time and financial support for the success of these projects.[27] Moreover, The College of Medical Evangelists (now Loma Linda University) in California contributed financially to this enterprise.[28]

Devotional exercises for patients, hospital staff, and some older members of the community were held in the AMH Chapel that was located on the hospital property. The chapel was "a barn-like structure with the lower half of the walls made of block and steel, while the upper half was of wire mesh."[29]

The original Andrews Memorial Hospital Chapel.
Photo: Courtesy of Andrews Memorial Seventh-day Adventist Church, Kingston, Jamaica.

Early in 1945 while Ruth Munroe was organizing the AMH Department of Nursing Service, she proceeded to organize a pre-nursing class, give lectures at West Indian Training College in Mandeville, and develop AMH School of Nursing.[30] The applicants were required to have completed four years of high school[31] and hold the Senior Cambridge Certificate or its equivalent.[32] Seven young ladies were accepted into the first class[33] and for three months[34] had special pre-nursing instruction under Munroe.[35] The programme of instruction included lectures on anatomy, physiology, chemistry, bacteriology, and public health concepts.[36] Social sciences and humanities were also part of the curriculum, but religion needed to be added.[37]

On May 6, 1945, the students were accepted as probationary nurses at AMH. The students were given lectures and demonstrations on the art and science of nursing along with instruction on the care of patients and on the preparation of food.[38] After successfully passing four months of pre-clinical studies, each student received her nurse's cap in a ceremony at the North Street Seventh-day Adventist Church.[39] The students then began thirty-six months of clinical instruction and clinical experiences at AMH and Andrews Memorial Clinic to become professional general nurses.[40] Thus, the first Seventh-day Adventist hospital school of nursing in the Inter-American Division was inaugurated.[41]

Beginning with the second group of students, the three months of pre-nursing instruction that had been taught at West Indian Training College were now taught at AMH.[42] The six months of pre-nursing instruction and pre-clinical studies included fifteen hours per week on the hospital wards.[43]

In 1946, the Jamaican government recognized AMH School of Nursing. This meant that the students were eligible to sit for the government examinations.[44] According to Ouida E. Spleen Westney, PhD, MSc, BSNE, RN, Class of 1950, a government examination was administered at the end of each clinical year. Upon successful performance of the third (final) examination, the Government Medical Department, Kingston, Jamaica, issued a certificate stating that the individual "passed the Examination of the Jamaica Examining Board for Nurses." When the Nursing Council of Jamaica was established in 1952, the Council provided documentation to those who had previously received such a certificate stating that they could use the "title of Registered Nurse."[45]

> *The students then began thirty-six months of clinical instruction and clinical experiences at AMH and Andrews Memorial Clinic to become professional general nurses. Thus, the first Seventh-day Adventist hospital school of nursing in the Inter-American Division was inaugurated.*

On August 27, 1946, Ruth Munroe and her father returned to the United States.[46] Her mother, who also contributed to the medical work in Kingston, had left Jamaica earlier in the year.[47] Clarence Munroe was a committed and earnest worker who gave valuable care to the patients and provided the supervision needed to transform Sulgrave Manor into AMH. Ruth Munroe was a faithful missionary nurse who was dedicated to advancing the health ministry of the church through knowledgeable and competent nursing care. After spending time on furlough, Ruth Munroe, who had been on loan to the British West Indies Union Mission, returned to the Far Eastern Division of Seventh-day Adventists to continue her service in Thailand (then Siam).[48] Upon her departure from Jamaica, F. Ruth Mitchell, BA, RN, of California[49] became the hospital matron[50] and director of the school of nursing.[51]

By October 1946, plans to build a new hospital had been approved by the AMH Board of Directors and the Inter-American Division of Seventh-day Adventists. The plans were in the process of being considered by the Kingston and St. Andrew Corporation for final disposition.[54]

On November 3, 1946,[55] ground was broken in front of Sulgrave Manor at 27 Hope Road.[56] A cornerstone was laid for a two-story concrete building of twenty-one rooms[57] that would become a general, acute hospital.[58]

In 1947, construction of the hospital was slow and actually stopped for a while due to insufficient funds.[59] However, the workers on the staff of AMH slowly moved forward by faith "praying that God would open the way to complete most of the main building and wings."[60]

Sister Carroll, who was a nurse administrator at Andrews Memorial Hospital; Ruth Mitchell, who was the second matron of Andrews Memorial Hospital and director of Andrews Memorial Hospital School of Nursing; and Sister Marjorie Whitney, who was the third hospital matron and director of the school of nursing.
Photo: Andrews Memorial Hospital Photograph Album, AMHPA-I-44-2, Department of Archives and Special Collections, Loma Linda University, Loma Linda, California.

At the end of 1947 and beginning of 1948, Gibson, the business manager, and B. M. Heald, who was on loan from the New York Conference, led a fund-raising campaign.[61] Moreover, everyone was encouraged when the Government of Jamaica appropriated funds for the hospital building project. With much gratitude to God, construction of the hospital continued at a faster pace.[62]

When the administrative and surgical wings of the main building were completed, the new AMH was officially opened on January 25, 1949, by His Excellency the Governor of Jamaica, Office of the British Empire,[63] Sir John Huggins.[64] The hospital, which previously had twenty beds,[65] now had forty beds for in-patients.[66]

*The new Andrews Memorial Hospital with the administrative and surgical wings
completed prior to its official opening in 1949.*
Photo: *Andrews Memorial Hospital Photograph Album, AMHPA-I-85-2, Department of Archives and
Special Collections, Loma Linda University, Loma Linda, California.*

*His Excellency the Governor of Jamaica, Office of the British Empire, Sir John Huggins speaking at
the opening ceremony of the new Andrews Memorial Hospital on January 25, 1949. The Union Jack
flag drapes the lectern. Other platform participants, left to right: Dr. Arthur William Nigel Druitt,
physician at Andrews Memorial Hospital; Dr. Theodore R. Flaiz, director, Medical Department,
General Conference of Seventh-day Adventists; Dr. Clifford R. Anderson, medical director, Andrews
Memorial Hospital; Mr. William Alexander Clarke Bustamante,
influential Jamaican leader; and unidentified gentleman.*
Photo: *Andrews Memorial Hospital Photograph Album, AMHPA-I-88-1, Department of Archives and
Special Collections, Loma Linda University, Loma Linda, California.*

It was desirous, of course, to finish the hospital building as quickly as possible. Dr. Anderson wrote an appeal titled, "Your Hospital Needs You," asking the Seventh-day Adventist church members in Jamaica to give whatever they could.[67] Furthermore, the government generously issued another grant to help finish construction of the hospital's east wing.[68]

While much attention was being given to the hospital building programme, it was in 1948 that major discussions ensued regarding the AMH and Clinic School of Nursing. The AMH Board of Directors voted to make some curricular changes and to increase the pre-nursing phase of instruction to one school year (two semesters).[69] The West Indian Training College Board of Management voted that they would add the pre-nursing course of study to the college curriculum as of January 4, 1949.[70] The AMH Board of Directors decided that Marjorie Whitney, BSc, RN, who was a faculty member in the school of nursing, would oversee the pre-nursing course of study in Mandeville.[71] Whitney had been supervisor of medical nursing at Loma Linda Sanitarium and Hospital in California,[72] but more recently had been superintendent of nurses at Montemorelos Hospital and Sanitarium in Mexico.[73] The AMH Board of Directors also voted that only those students who completed the pre-nursing course of study at West Indian Training College would be admitted to the school of nursing in January 1950.[74] Upon successful completion of thirty-six months of general nursing education, they would graduate and receive their diplomas from AMH and Clinic School of Nursing.[75]

Early in 1949, Dr. Anderson returned to the United States to join his wife who had departed Jamaica a few weeks previously due to ill health. Anderson devoted almost five years of his life in "wholehearted service" to promote the medical work in Jamaica.[76]

Launching such major health ministry initiatives was not easy. When Anderson began the building programme, he commented, "Breaking new ground is always difficult, often beset by discouragements. Our faith and patience were sorely tried on numerous occasions ... New paths are often rough, but we thank God for the many evidences of His leading and for the loyal help and confidence of our fellow workers both in the Hospital and in all the other branches of our work."[77]

Gibson and family also departed Jamaica.[78] After giving relentless effort in helping to develop the hospital, he accepted a call to be president of the Bahamas Mission.[79]

With the departure of Dr. Anderson, Dr. A. W. N. Druitt, who was from England and had worked with Anderson for more than two years,[80] was appointed medical director.[81] B. R. Hamilton, a Jamaican national,[82] was appointed business manager.[83] Under their leadership and that of Matron Mitchell, the building of a children's ward as an extension of Andrews Memorial Clinic on James Street was completed in December 1949. Building a children's ward was possible because during the previous two years, the Kingston and St. Andrew Corporation had given grants to the clinic in recognition of the charity services rendered there.[84]

Druitt, Mitchell, and Hamilton also started a clinic in Port Maria, St. Mary Parish, with the intent that this would be the first of several country clinics to be established in different areas of the island.[85] Unfortunately, the clinic was eventually closed due to a lack of financial resources.[86]

Beginning in 1950 and for the next two years, there were changes in the hospital administration. Mitchell went on furlough and decided not to return to Jamaica. She had already received several calls to connect with other Seventh-day Adventist medical institutions. Dr. Druitt remarked that "the Andrews Memorial Hospital owes a big debt of gratitude to her for unstinting service that she has so willingly given."[87] Marjorie Whitney was appointed the hospital matron and director of the school of nursing.[88] Druitt resigned as medical director but remained on staff for several months until he, too, went on furlough. Dr. E. J. Horsley of California was the medical director for only one year.[89] Subsequently, Dr. A. R. Parchment, a Jamaican national,[90] was appointed acting medical director.[91]

During Dr. Parchment's time in office, the hospital was completed in 1951 and had fifty-six beds for patients.[92] In addition to the administrative and surgical wings, the hospital had medical and obstetrical departments, a clinical laboratory and X-ray facilities, a pharmacy, a hydrotherapy department, offices for physicians, kitchen facilities, an area for out-patient services, and a building to do the laundry.[93] A portico connected the new hospital with the old hospital that had originally been Sulgrave Manor.[94]

Unfortunately, it was also in 1951 that Andrews Memorial Clinic had to be closed[95] due to a shortage of medical personnel.[96] Whatever could be moved was transferred to the hospital on Hope Road. From then on, the hospital and clinic functioned as one institution.[97]

In 1952, Dr. Martin Hoehn of New Brunswick, Canada,[98] arrived in Jamaica to assume the responsibilities of medical director.[99] Whitney continued as the hospital matron and director of the school of nursing.[100] Curtis Parchment, a Jamaican national,[101] was now the business manager.[102]

As of February 11, 1954,[103] D. Lois Burnett, MA, RN,[104] associate secretary for Nursing Education and Nursing Service, Medical Department, General Conference of Seventh-day Adventists, arrived in Jamaica.[105] During her consultation visit with Dr. Hoehn and Matron Whitney, she learned that in January 1953, the school of nursing was closed because the hospital's patronage did not increase sufficiently to provide adequate clinical experiences for the student nurses. Also, the University College Hospital School of Nursing had opened under the control of the University of London. Moreover, Kingston School of Nursing, the Teaching Department of Kingston Public Hospital, offered a programme to prepare general nurses.[106] Throughout the school's eight years of existence, the AMH Board of Directors issued diplomas to thirty-seven young ladies who were prepared to practice as professional general nurses.[107]

Although the general nurse diploma programme had been closed, the AMH School of Assistant Nursing (assistant enrolled nurse programme) was opened in 1954 under the direction of Matron Whitney and Dr. Hoehn.[108] Unfortunately due to health reasons,[109] Whitney returned to her home in California a year later after serving almost eight years in Jamaica.[110] She was honoured for her many contributions to nursing education and practice by the AMH administration and staff as well as her last class of assistant enrolled student nurses.[111]

In 1956, Ethel Heisler, RN, of Saskatchewan, Canada, succeeded Whitney as the hospital matron and director of the school of assistant nursing. Her husband, Edward J. Heisler, was appointed business manager.[112] It was also time to hire a full-time chaplain for AMH and a full time pastor for AMH Chapel.[113] On March 27, 1956, Pastor Owen P. Reid,[114] a Jamaican national,[115] accepted the call to serve in both positions.[116]

On June 26, 1956, the first Andrews Memorial Hospital Day was held. Prominent dignitaries and the general public were given a tour of the hospital. Aspects of health promotion were presented and the Adventist magazine, *Listen*, was distributed. The government dignitaries—His Excellency Sir Hugh Foot, Governor of Jamaica; Sir Alexander Bustamante, Leader of the Opposition; and the Honourable C. L. A. Stuart, Minister of Health,—expressed "pleasure at seeing such a fine hospital come to reality, high regard for the work that Andrews Memorial Hospital had provided through the years, and appreciation for helping to meet the need for medical care," respectively.[117]

In mid-1957, Dr. Hoehn left Jamaica to go on furlough and then do advanced training for fifteen months.[118] Dr. Leon Rittenhouse from the United States was medical director until the end of 1958.[119] When Hoehn returned to Jamaica, he served as a staff physician.[120]

In February 1959, Dr. G. H. A. McLaren of Australia and his family arrived in Jamaica. Dr. McLaren was the new medical director.[121] In August, Shirley Spain, BSc, RN, of Spokane, Washington,[122] became the hospital matron and director of the school of assistant nursing.[123] Heisler continued as business manager.[124] As is true of any institution, building improvements were made. Two examination rooms were remodelled for a new nursery, and the area for the old nursery was converted into a new pharmacy. Renovations were done to provide a more efficient working space for the nurses' station, and the clinical reception area was rearranged for better use. Not to be left unsaid, the delivery room was now air-conditioned.[125]

In 1961, Dr. McLaren and his family returned to Australia.[126] That same year, Matron Spain married Ellsworth Gallimore, a Jamaican national. A few months later, Shirley Spain Gallimore resigned as the hospital matron and director of the school of assistant nursing.[127] AMH continued to provide valuable health care to the people of Jamaica under the leadership of Dr. B. G. Arellano of California,[128] medical director;[129] Mildred Henry, BSc, RN, CM (certified midwife), who was a Jamaican national[130] and stepped up to be acting matron[131] then matron and director of the school of assistant nursing;[132] and Heisler, business manager.[133] Pastor Keith O. Boyd, a Jamaican national,[134] was the hospital chaplain and the pastor at AMH Chapel.[135]

Under Boyd's leadership, the new AMH Chapel was built. On April 24, 1966, it was ready to use for religious and community services. The old chapel became the hospital laundry building.[136]

In the late 1960s, the wards in the old section of AMH (formerly Sulgrave Manor) were closed[137] due to the fact that the manor was no longer a safe facility for patient care.[138] This decision reduced the hospital's number of beds from fifty-one in 1966[139] to thirty by 1968.[140] However, the first floor of the building was still used for clinical services.[141] At the time (1968), Dr. Mark W. Fowler of Georgia, USA,[142] was medical director;[143] Mildred Henry continued as the matron and director of the school of assistant nursing;[144] and Roy L. Henrickson of Portland, Oregon,[145] was business manager.[146] Pastor N. H. Thorpe, a Jamaican national,[147] was now the hospital chaplain.[148]

The new Andrews Memorial Hospital Chapel.
Photo: Courtesy of Andrews Memorial Seventh-day Adventist Church, Kingston, Jamaica.

Through the years, AMH personnel provided health education programmes, giving health talks in schools and churches as well as participating in community health rallies throughout the island.[149] Moreover, during Dr. Fowler's tenure as medical director, the AMH annual food fair included health aspects for the first time and was advertised as the International Food and Health Fair which was held on the hospital grounds. The AMH Auxiliary Association organized this event as a fund-raising project in order to provide essential items for the hospital. Only vegetarian meals, a recommended dietary practice of the Seventh-day Adventist church, were on the menu and represented a variety of cultures. There were also booths where one could purchase delectable sweets, fresh produce, health food products, decorative plants, and portraits drawn by a professional artist. Diabetes detection, tetanus inoculations, information on cancer as well as weight control, and a baby food demonstration were services provided without charge.[150]

> *The administration and staff at AMH embraced this commission to provide a health ministry in cooperation with divine power to bring physical, emotional, and spiritual healing to those who came for care.*

It was also in 1968 that the AMH Board of Directors made an organizational change relative to nursing service and nursing education. Mildred Henry had given excellent leadership as the hospital matron and director of the school of assistant nursing. However, the AMH Board of Directors decided it would be more effective to have the matron focus only on nursing service and to appoint someone else to be director of the school of assistant nursing.[151] Henry continued as the hospital matron.[152] In August 1968, Rebecca Gucilatar, BSc, RN, of the Philippines received a call from the General Conference of Seventh-day Adventists to be director of the AMH School of Assistant Nursing.[153] Gucilatar would begin her new position in early 1969.[154]

Beginning the health work in Jamaica was in accordance with the Seventh-day Adventist denomination's belief that the church has a responsibility to provide health care and teach health principles. "The healing ministry of Christ was seen to be a manifestation of divine love which should be continued in the world through the instrumentality of the church."[155] The administration and staff at AMH embraced this commission to provide a health ministry in cooperation with divine power to bring physical, emotional, and spiritual healing to those who came for care. Their mission of loving service would continue long into the future for the people of Jamaica and the West Indies.

CHAPTER 4

Baccalaureate Nursing Education—Beginnings

On February 11, 1969, Rebecca Gucilatar, BSc, RN, arrived in Kingston, Jamaica, to be director of Andrews Memorial Hospital (AMH) School of Assistant Nursing.[1] She was also a member of the AMH Board of Directors. However, within a matter of time an additional endeavour would be awaiting her expertise in nursing education.

During her first few months in Jamaica, Miss Gucilatar observed that there were enrolled assistant nurse students in her classroom as well as applicants seeking admission to the AMH School of Assistant Nursing who possessed intellectual abilities and other attributes that would enable them to successfully achieve the degree, bachelor of science in nursing. Thus, Gucilatar began to inquire about types of nursing programmes offered in Kingston, Jamaica.[2] At the time, there were hospital-based programmes to prepare enrolled assistant nurses and general nurses.[3] Gucilatar learned that prominent nurse leaders in Jamaica had "a supreme desire to establish" a baccalaureate nursing programme for those who resided in Jamaica and the Caribbean region.[4] However, launching such an initiative was still in the future.

As of July 1969, Dr. Mark Fowler, who had been the medical director at AMH, returned to the United States. Dr. Charles Wilkens, a staff physician, became interim medical director until April 30, 1970. He then went on furlough to do a surgical residency.[5] Subsequently, Dr. Basil C. Arthur, a cardiothoracic surgeon of Los Angeles, California, accepted the call to be a relief physician on a short-term basis beginning in May 1970. Four years previously he had served as a relief physician at AMH.[6, 7]

Upon Dr. Arthur's arrival in Jamaica, Miss Gucilatar shared with him that she wanted to develop a four-year, baccalaureate nursing programme. He conveyed genuine interest in her desire to take on such an endeavour and suggested that she design a scheme for such a programme.[8]

Kenneth G. Vaz, president of West Indies College (WIC), had done some preliminary work in 1969 regarding a baccalaureate nursing programme.[9] However, most of the work was yet to be accomplished under the leadership of Gucilatar, who was an experienced staff nurse, nurse administrator, and nurse educator.[10]

Rebecca Gucilatar immediately took up the mantle and began the process that would result in a four-year, baccalaureate nursing programme. She was well-versed in the Adventist educational model of preparing quality nurses in the setting of a tertiary educational institution. She also had a comprehensive understanding of the Adventist philosophy of whole person care that includes meeting the spiritual needs of the patient. However, she had never initiated development of a collegiate department of nursing education.[11] Thus, Gucilatar began seeking consultations from nurse leaders whom she knew in the Far Eastern Division and the North American Division of Seventh-day Adventists, deans of Seventh-day Adventist schools of nursing, and Mazie A. Herin, MN, RN, associate secretary for nursing education and nursing service, Medical Department, General Conference of Seventh-day Adventists. She also held meetings with several nurse leaders in Jamaica to learn about requirements to practice general nursing in Jamaica, government regulations, and the necessary steps to proceed with such an endeavour.[12]

Gucilatar's next step was to become knowledgeable about the philosophy, beliefs, and goals of WIC. She learned that they were similar to other Seventh-day Adventist educational institutions of higher learning throughout the world. Thus, the theoretical framework for nursing education that Gucilatar wrote and the curriculum that she designed were in alignment with other Seventh-day Adventist baccalaureate nursing programmes. The curriculum included course content that met baccalaureate degree requirements of WIC as well as course content and clinical experiences that met requirements stipulated by the Nursing Council of Jamaica.[13]

The programme that Gucilatar designed underwent several revisions. This was not unusual for a new initiative of this kind. However, she experienced a time of discouragement due to feelings of isolation in the work she was doing. Although Dr. Arthur and others were close by supporting her endeavours, key advisors and consultants were "at distant places." She wrote, "Long-distance calls, telegrams, and letters from them boosted my spirit in the planning."[14]

The scheme for the baccalaureate nursing programme was finally ready for presentation. Gucilatar organized and chaired a steering committee to examine what she had written and to assist with the planning of this new programme. Other AMH committee members were Dr. Arthur; Mildred Henry, matron; Alton B. Marshalleck, business manager; and R. Dyke, supervisor of the clinical laboratory. After the committee reviewed Gucilatar's proposal, they considered the following points:

(1) the nursing programme be a department of WIC,
(2) the chairman of the programme have a master's degree [in nursing] and preferably a doctoral degree,
(3) the faculty be academically qualified with a bachelor of science degree [in nursing] or a master's degree in a specialty area of nursing, and
(4) the programme be approved by the General Conference of Seventh-day Adventists Department of Education, the Nursing Council of Jamaica, and the Jamaica Government's Ministry of Health.[15]

Miss Gucilatar wrote, "I observed a spirit of willingness and cooperation. There was a spirit of oneness in the idea and plan of implementation."[16]

At this point, the steering committee deemed it essential to contact educators and church leaders for their involvement and approval. Those contacted were Colin D.

Standish, PhD, academic dean who would soon become president of WIC; Pastor H. S. Walters, president of the West Indies Union Conference; Pastor L. Herbert Fletcher, educational secretary of the West Indies Union Conference; Charles R. Taylor, PhD, secretary of the Inter-American Division of Seventh-day Adventists Department of Education; Charles B. Hirsch, PhD, General Conference of Seventh-day Adventists Department of Education; and Mazie A. Herin, who was already serving as a consultant. The Nursing Council of Jamaica and the Ministry of Health were also contacted.[17]

The next step was to organize a planning committee to develop operational criteria for the programme. Fletcher was the chairman. Other members were Walters, Standish, Arthur, Gucilatar, Henry, and Marshalleck. The criteria were as follows:

(1) WIC was to incorporate a Department of Nursing Education,
(2) the baccalaureate nursing programme was to be administered by the designated chairman of the Department of Nursing Education,
(3) a budget for the department was to be developed separately from the budget for AMH,
(4) recruitment of academically qualified faculty was to be done immediately,
(5) negotiations were to be done to obtain approval from the Nursing Council of Jamaica and the Ministry of Health,
(6) the plan to expand AMH was to start immediately to meet the required bed capacity of 100+ by 1973–1974, and
(7) the nursing programme was to be implemented.[18]

It was understood that WIC would implement the baccalaureate nursing programme in affiliation with AMH. However, due to financial constraints, WIC was not able to support the clinical phase of the programme without the assistance of AMH. Thus, Walters as president of the West Indies Union Conference requested that AMH initially support the clinical phase of the baccalaureate nursing programme. The AMH Board of Directors voted to financially assist in this endeavour for two years. It was also decided that the chairman's office for the WIC Department of Nursing Education be located at the AMH campus rather than the Mandeville campus. This decision was made because most of the health care facilities were in Kingston, and the chairman of the WIC baccalaureate nursing programme would continue to be director of the AMH School of Assistant Nursing.[19]

> *"I observed a spirit of willingness and cooperation. There was a spirit of oneness in the idea and plan of implementation."*

A negotiation committee was then formed to obtain approval from the different levels of the church's organization, the Nursing Council of Jamaica, and the Ministry of Health. Members of this committee were Walters, Fletcher, Gucilatar, Arthur, and Marshalleck.[20]

Exercising much faith, an admissions committee was also formed by early summer of 1970. Members of this committee representing WIC were: Dr. Standish, who was now president of the college; Hermon L. Douce, PhD, academic dean;

Lucille Walters, MA, registrar; and Robert T. Andrews, PhD, faculty member. Those who represented AMH were Rebecca Gucilatar, Matron Henry, Dr. Arthur, and Alton Marshalleck. This group of individuals immediately began interviewing applicants for admission to the baccalaureate nursing programme.[21]

In the meantime, Miss Gucilatar met with Julie Symes, registrar, Nursing Council of Jamaica, and presented the curricula to her for the Council to consider.[22] The Council has legal jurisdiction to stipulate the curriculum for basic training courses in general nursing and to require that three years of general clinical nursing be completed in order to sit the national examination (now regional examination) to become a registered general nurse.[23] The Council did not give an immediate decision.[24] However, after Gucilatar discussed the curricula with Symes, it was apparent that the three years of professional nursing courses outlined in the WIC curriculum would meet the Council's requirements.[25] In good faith, the WIC Board of Trustees, the West Indies Union Executive Committee, the Inter-American Division Department of Education, and the General Conference Department of Education voted to implement the bachelor of science degree programme in nursing that was projected to begin fall semester 1970. In June 1970, Rebecca Gucilatar was appointed as the first chairman of WIC Department of Nursing Education.[26]

CHAPTER 5

Rebecca Gucilatar-Jakobsen

Rebecca Gucilatar-Jakobsen, Chairman
West Indies College Department of Nursing Education
1970 to 1971 and 1973 to 1976
Photo: Courtesy of Southern Asia-Pacific Division of Seventh-day Adventists.

Rebecca Gucilatar's early education began on the island of Polillo in the province of Quezon, Philippines. Later, she obtained her BSc degree in nursing from Philippine Union College (now Adventist University of the Philippines) in affiliation with Manila Sanitarium and Hospital. After graduating from college, Gucilatar was a staff nurse and then an assistant head nurse at Manila Sanitarium and Hospital.[1]

In 1962, Miss Gucilatar accepted a call to serve at the Benghazi Adventist Hospital in Libya, Africa.[2] Two years later, she was appointed acting director of nurses.[3] In 1966, she returned to the Philippines.[4] For the next three years, Gucilatar was an instructor at Philippine Union College School of Nursing[5] and acting dean of residence.[6]

In 1969, Gucilatar accepted the call to go to Jamaica to be director of the Andrews Memorial Hospital School of Assistant Nursing.[7] Moreover, she soon became involved in developing West Indies College (WIC) Department of Nursing Education and implementing the initial stages of the baccalaureate nursing programme.[8] Rebecca Gucilatar was the first Filipino missionary from the Far East to serve in the Inter-American Division of Seventh-day Adventists.[9, 10]

In 1971, the Inter-American Division granted Gucilatar an educational leave of absence to obtain a MSc degree in nursing from Loma Linda University, a Seventh-day Adventist institution in California.[11, 12] She then returned to Jamaica in 1973 to resume her role as chairman of WIC Department of Nursing Education.[13]

In 1974, Miss Gucilatar met Kresten Jakobsen, whom she married on March 30, 1975. The following year in August 1976, they moved to California where Rebecca Gucilatar-Jakobsen held positions in nursing at various health care facilities including Loma Linda University Medical Center and Loma Linda Veterans Administration Medical Center.[14]

"She was devoted to enhancing the academic needs and welfare of those outside of her cultural community."

Mrs. Gucilatar-Jakobsen enjoyed writing. While in Jamaica she wrote a poem titled, "When You Become a Nurse." The poem was included in the *AMH School of Assistant Nursing Bulletin*.[15] After returning to the United States, she wrote another poem titled, "A Crown of Glory," that was published in the *College Voice* (now *University Voice*), the official journal of Adventist University of the Philippines Student Association.[16]

Some of the baccalaureate graduates whom Rebecca Gucilatar-Jakobsen taught remembered her as "enthusiastic," "very determined," "got things done," "a good role model," "kind-hearted," and "spiritual." One graduate said, "She expected the best in us," and another graduate commented, "She was a live wire constantly receiving new insights and solutions." Yet another graduate remarked, "She was devoted to enhancing the academic needs and welfare of those outside of her cultural community."[17]

Mrs. Gucilatar-Jakobsen retired in 2002. She and her husband then moved from California to Minnesota. After so many years of dedication to the nursing profession, Rebecca Gucilatar-Jakobsen died unexpectedly on October 19, 2006.[18]

CHAPTER 6

Doors Open Wide

The summer of 1970 saw a change in leadership at West Indies College (WIC) and Andrews Memorial Hospital (AMH). In June 1970, President Vaz participated in his last commencement event before retiring from WIC.[1] Colin D. Standish, PhD, who was academic dean and head of the Department of Education,[2] was appointed the next president of WIC.[3] Hermon L. Douce, PhD, was appointed academic dean.[4]

On July 10, 1970, Dr. Herbert Holness and his family, of San Diego, California, arrived in Kingston, Jamaica.[5] He was acting medical director at AMH for two years[6] before accepting the position of medical director for the next six years.[7]

It was also a summer going full speed ahead with continued planning, negotiations, and student recruitment. The stories of how the young people learned about this new model of a four-year, baccalaureate nursing programme are examples of how God was leading in their lives and this endeavour. One individual had been accepted at a hospital school of nursing in Jamaica and a hospital school of nursing in England. She was at the WIC Commencement in June 1970 and heard President Vaz's announcement about starting a baccalaureate nursing programme. She immediately applied to WIC. As she said, "I wanted to attend a Seventh-day Adventist college where I could sit and soak up spiritual experiences."

> "I wanted to attend a Seventh-day Adventist college where I could sit and soak up spiritual experiences."

She was present on the first day of classes. Likewise, another individual had been accepted at a hospital school of nursing in Jamaica, but her mother wanted her to be in a Seventh-day Adventist environment. With a quick phone call to Lucille Walters, the WIC registrar, the daughter was in classes the next day. Another young lady wanted to be a physical therapist but was too young to be admitted to such a programme. She then learned about the baccalaureate nursing programme offered at WIC and chose to major in nursing.[8]

Others learned about the new nursing programme by being on the WIC campus. One young lady was a senior in the high school division of WIC. She wanted to be a teacher, but there were some factors that deterred her. She then heard the "buzz" on campus about the new nursing programme. She tried nursing and "grew to love it."[9]

By September 1970, ten students began their freshman year of pre-nursing studies at WIC in Mandeville.[10] For the next twelve months they took courses in biological, natural, and social sciences; Christian Faith; College Algebra; English Composition; Health Education; and Principles of Education.[11]

On January 29, 1971, Julie Symes, on behalf of the Nursing Council of Jamaica, sent a letter to Alton Marshalleck, business manager at AMH, regarding the BSc degree programme in nursing. Symes wrote to him that "The Council considered the scheme an experimental one breaking quite new ground in Jamaica as a method to prepare nurses for the Register. The Council approved the second, third, and fourth years of the course only. It was felt that the instructions given in these years equated with the three year diploma courses for the Register which were conducted at the Kingston and the University Hospital Schools of Nursing."[12] Provisional approval was granted to the WIC Department of Nursing Education.[13] "The provisional approval was given on the premise that clinical experiences in psychiatric and paediatric nursing would be accessed in government hospitals, which AMH did not provide."[14]

Although AMH was the parent hospital in affiliation with WIC for the baccalaureate nursing programme, it was a small hospital and could accommodate the student nurses only for the sophomore year of required clinical experiences. Thus, Rebecca Gucilatar began discussions with the administrators of government-operated health care institutions to obtain clinical experiences for the junior year of the programme. However, Gucilatar was denied access.[15]

Known for his perseverance, Pastor Walters met with Enid Lawrence, RN, CM, principal tutor, University Hospital of the West Indies School of Nursing, Mona, and Norma Woodham, RN, CM, tutor. Walters sought their assistance to obtain clinical experiences at the University Hospital of the West Indies, a quasi-government hospital owned by the Caribbean Islands. Lawrence and Woodham were extremely supportive of WIC establishing a baccalaureate nursing programme. With their assistance and with permission of the matron (name not given), and the hospital administrator (name not given), doors opened for the WIC student nurses to gain clinical experiences at University Hospital of the West Indies. This arrangement was initially done on friendly terms.[16] Later, when Lois Dujon became the matron, she, too, gave her support.

Enid Lawrence, principal tutor at University Hospital of the West Indies School of Nursing (UHWISON). In 1974, Lawrence became Director of Nursing Education at UHWISON.

Norma Woodham, tutor at University Hospital of the West Indies School of Nursing.

Lois Dujon, administrator of UHWISON and matron of the hospital from 1972–1974. Dujon then became director of nursing service at University Hospital of the West Indies.

Photos: reproduced by permission of the publisher from A Road to Excellence: The History of Basic Nursing Education at the University Hospital of the West Indies, Jamaica, 1949–2006 by Claire Duncan, Valerie Hardware, Jean Munroe and Norma Woodham (Kingston: Canoe Press, 2017), 215, 216, and 214, respectively. Biographical information is on pages 213–217.

Furthermore, Lawrence and Woodham were instrumental in assisting Gucilatar to obtain clinical experiences at government-operated health care facilities in Kingston. With their support and guidance, Gucilatar had discussions with the matrons and medical directors of various government hospitals to use their facilities for the WIC student nurses. There were also discussions with Laurice Hunter-Scott, RN, Principal Nursing Officer (now Chief Nursing Officer) which is the highest position in nursing in the Ministry of Health. Once again, arrangements were made on a friendly basis as the Ministry of Health did not formally approve through written contracts that WIC student nurses could use government-operated health care facilities.[17]

In the spring of 1971, Miss Gucilatar prepared information for the *WIC Bulletin 1971–1972* academic year. It was the first time the bulletin included a section on the WIC Department of Nursing Education and its affiliation with AMH. Prerequisites, some of the faculty, the original four-year curriculum, and course descriptions were included in the bulletin. Clinical facilities such as University Hospital of the West Indies and some of the government-operated health care facilities were also listed.[18]

In June 1971, Rebecca Gucilatar temporarily left Jamaica for a three-month furlough and then to begin study towards a graduate degree in nursing.[19] As indicated in her proposal for the WIC baccalaureate nursing programme, the chairman was to have at least a master's degree, a degree she did not have herself.[20] This criterion was in accordance with the General Conference of Seventh-day Adventists Executive Committee who was calling workers with higher qualifications to be administrators of professional programmes in educational institutions of higher learning.[21] Thus, she was granted an educational leave to obtain a MSc degree in nursing at Loma Linda University in California.[22, 23]

Knowing that Rebecca Gucilatar would be going on educational leave, Elder J. H. Figueroa Jr., secretary of the Inter-American Division of Seventh-day Adventists, forwarded a request to Elder T. H. Baasch, associate secretary of the General Conference of Seventh-day Adventists, for someone to temporarily fill Gucilatar's position. Elder Baasch, in turn, requested that David J. Bieber, EdD, president of Loma Linda University, and Marilyn J. Christian, EdDc, RN, dean of Loma Linda University School of Nursing, provide a school of nursing faculty member to serve as acting chairman for the next two years. President Bieber and Dean Christian agreed to meet this need of the Inter-American Division of Seventh-day Adventists, WIC, and AMH.[24]

CHAPTER 7

Colin D. Standish

Colin D. Standish, President
West Indies College
1970 to 1973
Photo: Courtesy of Northern Caribbean University.

Colin David Standish[1] and an identical twin brother, Russell, were born on October 27, 1933, to Darcy Rowland Standish and Hilda Marie Joyce Standish (née Bailey) in Newcastle, New South Wales, Australia. During their childhood years, they attended the Boolaroo and Cardiff public schools and then in 1943 attended Newcastle Adventist High School.

From January 1950 to December 1951, Standish studied at Australasian Missionary College (now Avondale College) in Cooranbong, New South Wales. He graduated having completed the course in primary teaching and the Theological Normal Course. From 1952 to 1954, he taught at Ophir Glen Adventist Elementary School in Burringbar,

New South Wales, followed by one year of teaching at Mullumbimby Adventist School in New South Wales.

At this point, Standish decided to further his education. He attended the University of Sydney in Australia and earned a BA, MA, and PhD in psychology. While a graduate student, he moved to Coogee, a beachside suburb of Sydney, to be a live-in residence dean at Legacy House. This was a place for college-age children of returned service men to live while they studied in Sydney. "Legacy is a charity providing services to Australian families suffering after the injury or death of a spouse or parent, during or after their defence force service."[2] Standish then began to attend the Woollahra Seventh-day Adventist Church in Sydney that was the home church of Cheryl Basham. Colin Standish and Miss Basham began to date and were married on August 29, 1963. He completed his doctoral degree in 1964.

In January 1965, Dr. Standish returned to his alma mater, Avondale College, to serve as chairman of the Department of Education. At the same time, he earned a master's degree in education from the University of Sydney. During his fifth year at Avondale College, Standish received a telephone call from H. S. Walters, president of the West Indies Union Conference. Walters asked Standish to be the academic dean at West Indies College (WIC, now Northern Caribbean University) in Mandeville, Jamaica. At the end of 1969, Dr. and Mrs. Standish left Australia en route to Jamaica.

On January 30, 1970, Standish began his work as academic dean at WIC. However, in only a few months Dr. Standish was elected president of the college until February 4, 1973. His wife Cheryl served as his secretary in both positions. While in Jamaica, Standish was ordained as a Seventh-day Adventist minister on April 17, 1971.

In early 1973, Dr. Standish accepted a call to Columbia Union College (now Washington Adventist University) in Maryland. After serving for a short period as chairman of the Department of Psychology and then academic dean, he was appointed president until June 1978. Dr. and Mrs. Standish then moved to California where he joined Weimar Institute of Health and Education and was founding dean of Weimar College for the next five years. During this time, they were blessed with a son, Nigel.

In 1983, Dr. Standish and his family moved to Rapidan, Virginia. Here, he founded and was president of Hartland Institute. Two years after moving to Virginia, Dr. and Mrs. Standish were blessed with a daughter, Alexandra. In 2011, Standish stepped down as president of Hartland Institute but continued to attend board meetings, teach courses, write, and accept speaking engagements.

Dr. Standish gave more than sixty-five years of his life to the cause of God. He espoused Biblical truths of Seventh-day Adventist Christianity in his roles of administrator, teacher, minister, world-wide speaker, and author. He and his brother, Russell, were prolific authors and published numerous books and articles defending the Adventist faith.

Colin David Standish retired on May 25, 2017. After a prolonged illness, he died on October 29, 2018.

Chapter 8

Herbert A. Holness

Herbert Holness, Medical Director
Andrews Memorial Hospital
1970 to 1978
Photo by Ron Nelson. Courtesy of Andrews Memorial Hospital.

Herbert Augustus Holness was born in Bocas del Toro, Panama, on January 29, 1918. His parents were from Jamaica, but at the time his father was working on the Panama Canal. Eventually, his father moved the family back to Jamaica.[1] From 1942 to 1945,[2] Holness attended West Indian Training College, Mandeville, Jamaica, and received his diploma having completed the Ministerial Course.[3] He then served as pastor of a Seventh-day Adventist Church in Jamaica during the summer of 1945.[4]

From September 1945 to July 1947, Holness attended Pacific Union College, a Seventh-day Adventist college in California.[5] He completed the Preparation for Medical Course curricula. This curricula enabled him to meet the required prerequisites to attend medical school at the College of Medical Evangelists (now Loma Linda University School of Medicine) in California.[6,7] He graduated in 1952 with the degree, doctor of medicine.[8] In the same year, Pacific Union College conferred on Holness the BA degree in medical science.[9]

Leaving California, Dr. Holness travelled to Nashville, Tennessee, and became a staff physician at Riverside Sanitarium and Hospital, a Seventh-day Adventist hospital. It was also his responsibility to do physical examinations at Oakwood College (now Oakwood University), a Seventh-day Adventist college in Huntsville, Alabama. While in Huntsville, he met Marcheta Valentine, who was teaching at Oakwood Academy. On June 1, 1955, Dr. Holness and Miss Valentine were married.[10]

Shortly after marriage, Dr. Holness received a commission to serve in the United States Army. Subsequently, Holness and his wife moved to France where he was stationed at the United States Army 34th General Hospital in La Chapelle-Saint-Mesmin until 1958. They then moved to San Diego, California, where Dr. Holness worked with Dr. John R. Ford at the Ford Medical Center until 1970. During this time, Holness was on the staff of Paradise Valley Hospital, a Seventh-day Adventist hospital, as well as other hospitals in the area. He was a member of the San Diego Medical Society. Dr. and Mrs. Holness had four children: Yvette, Robert, Ronald, and Roderick.[11]

In spite of broken ribs and being a patient himself, he put on his robe and made rounds in the hospital to check on the patients who were under his care.

In May 1970, the Inter-American Division of Seventh-day Adventists appointed Dr. Herbert A. Holness as acting medical director at Andrews Memorial Hospital (AMH). Holness responded a month later that he would accept the call "on a trial basis."[12] He and his family arrived in Jamaica on July 10, 1970.[13] For two years he was acting medical director[14] then agreed to serve as medical director for the next six years.[15]

In the summer of 1972, Dr. Holness was in an automobile accident in Kingston and was admitted to AMH. In spite of broken ribs and being a patient himself, he put on his robe and made rounds in the hospital to check on the patients who were under his care.[16]

In 1978, Dr. and Mrs. Holness returned to San Diego. For the next twelve years Holness worked with his brother-in-law, Dr. Jimmie Valentine, in the inner-city community. Holness and his wife then returned to Jamaica from 1990 to 1995 so that Dr. Holness could serve once again as a staff physician at AMH. Upon retiring, Holness and his wife lived in Highland, California, until his death on March 9, 2000.[17]

In honour of Dr. Holness, the AMH Outpatient Department was named "The Herbert Holness Clinic" on April 30, 2000. This was done "in appreciation of the many years of dedicated services given by Dr. Holness to this institution."[18] Those who worked with Dr. Holness in Jamaica would agree with a comment made by his daughter, Yvette Adrienne Holness, MD, "He loved his patients and he loved working at AMH."[19]

CHAPTER 9
Boldly Moving Forward

Kingston, the largest city in Jamaica and the capital of Jamaica, was bustling with energy in the early 1970s. There was a parliament forging ahead to build a strong, independent nation; ongoing expansion of business enterprises; development of more modern health care delivery systems; the constant flow of tourists; and the usual traffic jams. Off in the distance were the eternally beautiful Blue Mountains.

In July 1971, Antoinette Klingbeil, MSc, RN, accepted a call from the General Conference of Seventh-day Adventists to begin a one-year leave of absence from Loma Linda University to serve as acting chairman of West Indies College (WIC) Department of Nursing Education. She was also acting director of Andrews Memorial Hospital (AMH) School of Assistant Nursing and a member of the AMH Board of Directors. Mrs. Klingbeil taught in both nursing programmes as well. Her husband, Pastor Reinhold Klingbeil, MA, MSc, MPH, likewise, accepted a call to be the chaplain at AMH, pastor of AMH Chapel, and to teach in the WIC baccalaureate nursing programme.[1] However, the Klingbeils were unable to arrive in Kingston until September 26, 1971.[2]

In the meantime, the General Conference asked Erma L. Serles, RN, to temporarily go to Jamaica before the first batch (group or class) of students would arrive on the AMH campus to begin their sophomore year of college and the clinical phase of the baccalaureate nursing programme. She gladly accepted the opportunity to serve once again in Jamaica.[3] Serles was director of the Hinsdale Sanitarium and Hospital (now AMITA Health Adventist Medical Center Hinsdale) School of Practical Nursing in Illinois[4] and had previously been a relief nurse at AMH.[5]

Although ten students began their pre-nursing studies in 1970, only four of them entered the clinical phase of the nursing programme as of fall semester 1971.[6] It is known that some migrated to the United States to continue their studies in nursing, and some had not completed their pre-nursing courses.[7] There may have been other reasons.

Providentially, two students who had been enrolled in the arts and science programme at WIC decided to become nurses. One was a senior who was about to graduate in June 1971 with an associate degree. Lucille Walters, registrar, asked the student to come to her office. After discussing the student's future plans, Walters informed the student that she had completed prerequisite courses required for the baccalaureate nursing programme and encouraged the student to continue her quest for a bachelor's degree. The student chose to do it in nursing. The other student had completed one year in the arts and science programme with plans to be a doctor. However, she didn't know when, where, or how this would be financially possible.

She had observed "a lot of excitement about this new prestigious BSN [bachelor of science in nursing] programme." She decided to become a nurse in the summer of 1971. She remarked, "So happy I made the switch. It was definitely God's leading."[8]

The first batch of student nurses to enter the clinical phase of the baccalaureate nursing programme included Judith Clayton, Leonarda Dowdie, Sonia Kennedy, Shirlene McLean, Beverley McPherson, and Beverley Tai. They called themselves "The Big Six." Five of the students were from Jamaica, and one was from Grand Cayman Island.[9] When the students arrived at the AMH campus in early September, Serles began teaching some classes.[10] She also took the students to a store in uptown to be measured for their nursing uniforms and to place the order.[11]

> *She decided to become a nurse in the summer of 1971. She remarked, "So happy I made the switch. It was definitely God's leading."*

The fall semester of the sophomore year included courses on Foundations of Nursing, Basic Nutrition in Nursing, Introduction to Sociology, Human Relations in Nursing, Family Life, Ministry of Healing, and Health & Physical Education.[12] Space was at a premium. However, classrooms were made available on the second floor (Unit 200) of the old AMH (formerly Sulgrave Manor).[13] Classes were also held in rooms that were used for various church and community activities at AMH Chapel.[14] The basic nursing skills laboratory was in a small bungalow behind the business manager's house.[15]

The Basic Nursing Skills Laboratory was located in this small bungalow behind the business manager's house.
Photo by Lamoyjé Fletcher.

When the Klingbeils arrived in late September, Serles returned to the United States. In addition to teaching, Antoinette Klingbeil continued negotiations to secure clinical experiences at other hospitals for the junior year. Once again, Enid Lawrence and Norma Woodham were instrumental in assisting with these negotiations.[16] Reinhold Klingbeil assumed his responsibilities as chaplain, pastor, and teacher.[17]

The clinical assignments for the sophomore year were done at AMH. When the six student nurses were ready to begin taking care of patients, their uniforms were still being made. Thus, the temporary uniform was a white blouse, dark blue skirt, neutral-coloured nylon stockings, and white shoes.[18] Eventually, they wore the official uniform which was a one-piece, white bib and skirt worn over a pale blue, pin-stripe shift dress

The first class of six student nurses in their temporary uniforms standing with the matron of Andrews Memorial Hospital. Left to right: Judith Clayton, Shirlene McLean, Sonia Kennedy, Matron Mildred Henry, Beverley McPherson, Beverley Tai, and Leonarda Dowdie.
Photo: Courtesy of Sonia Kennedy-Brown.

The first class of six student nurses in their official uniforms standing with Mrs. Klingbeil, acting chairman of West Indies College Department of Nursing Education:
Left to right: Shirlene McLean, Judith Clayton, Beverley McPherson, Mrs. Klingbeil, Beverley Tai, Sonia Kennedy, and Leonarda Dowdie.
Photo: Courtesy of Sonia Kennedy-Brown.

with short, cuffed sleeves and a small collar. White nylon stockings and white shoes completed their uniform.[19]

In 1971, AMH had thirty hospital beds and an out-patient clinic. The medical and nursing personnel included Dr. Holness, acting medical director; three staff physicians; Mildred Henry, matron; and twelve staff nurses.[20] A royal poinciana tree with its fiery orange-red flowers, locally called "Flame of the Forest," was surrounded by shrubs of hibiscus in front of the main entrance to the hospital. Shrubs of hibiscus also lined the front of the hospital. The rest of the property was abundant with fruit-bearing trees such as ackee, Jamaica cherry, mango, sour apple, and tamarind.[21]

The front entrance to Andrews Memorial Hospital in 1972.
Photo by Karen J. Radke.

In addition to the hospital, other buildings had been renovated for a different use, erected, or purchased to expand the property at 27 Hope Road. The middle section of the first floor of the old AMH was used for the clinic. It was a large room that was partitioned into several areas so the physicians could examine the patients. West of the clinic on the first floor was an office for Antoinette Klingbeil just as there had been for

Facing the west end of the original Andrews Memorial Hospital as it appeared in 1972.
Offices were located on the first floor in the west end. The wards on the second floor were closed to the care of patients in the late 1960s. The building that housed the clinical laboratory and X-ray departments can be seen beyond the portico.
Photo by Karen J. Radke.

Rebecca Gucilatar; offices for business management personnel, medical records clerks, and public relations personnel; and an area to store medical records. East of the clinic on the first floor was the kitchen. In front of the old hospital was a walkway. When walking in an eastward direction, it connected to a concrete walkway which led to a concrete building that housed the clinical laboratory and X-ray departments. South of

Aerial view (1968) of Andrews Memorial Hospital in the foreground connecting via a portico to the original hospital. The hospitals faced north. The large, flat-roofed building east of the original hospital enclosed the clinical laboratory and X-ray departments. The small, flat-roofed building was the cafeteria.
Photo: Courtesy of Andrews Memorial Hospital and Alton B. Marshalleck, former business manager, who provided a print of the photograph. Source unknown.

this building was the cafeteria that served vegetarian food for patients, employees, student nurses, and visitors. Gladys Brodie, who was affectionately called "Aunt Glad," was head of the dietary department. Beyond the cafeteria and the old AMH was the laundry building and a large mango tree under which the ladies would soak some of the linens in large steel tubs and then hang them on clothes lines to dry.[22]

AMH Chapel was in the northeast corner of the property. Going south along the property line was a volleyball court, a duplex (living quarters) for hospital personnel such as "Aunt" Glad, and ongoing construction of the nurses' dormitory. Beyond the future dormitory was a house for one of the physicians and his family in the southeast corner of the property.[23]

West of the hospital were two houses owned by AMH. One was the business manager's residence at the corner of Hope Road and Phoenix Avenue. The house next door on Hope Road was used temporarily as a dormitory for the six student nurses and Rosella Nesbitt, residence hall dean.[24] On July 11, 1971, a groundbreaking ceremony had been held for the new dormitory. Dr. Basil C. Arthur was the "moving spirit" behind this project and donated liberally towards its success.[25] Although the AMH Board of Directors planned to have the nurses' dormitory ready for occupancy when the first class arrived in September, that was not possible because of a delay in construction.[26]

Gladys Brodie ("Aunt Glad"), head of Andrews
Memorial Hospital Dietary Department.
Photo by JoAnn Jones.

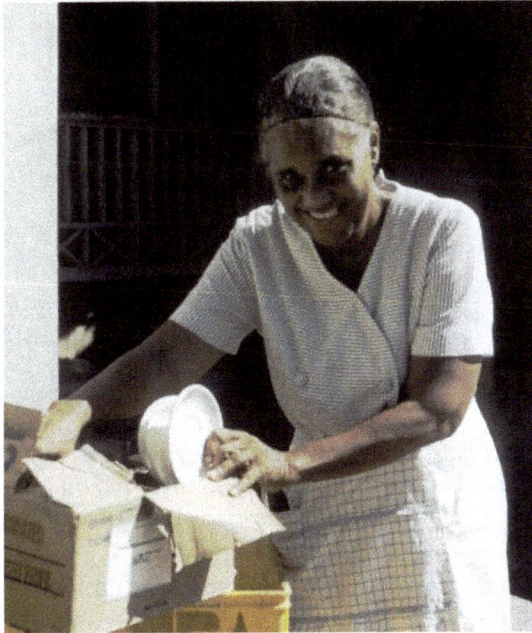

Miss Brodie unpacking dishes.
Photo by Karen J. Radke.

Rosella Nesbitt, residence hall dean on the Andrews Memorial Hospital campus.
Photo: Courtesy of Northern Caribbean University.

Beverley Tai and Beverley McPherson (left to right) relaxing on the terrace of the house on Hope Road
that served as the first women's dormitory for the student nurses.
Photo: Courtesy of Beverley McPherson.

The BSc degree programme in nursing was academically under the auspices of WIC. However, the college was not in a position to finance the clinical phase of the programme. Thus, during the planning phase of the programme, the AMH Board of Directors had voted to provide financial assistance from 1971 to 1973.[27]

AMH provided the use of its facilities and continued to engage in fund-raising to provide adequate accommodations for the student nurses. Moreover, AMH staff who had expertise to provide classroom teaching and/or clinical supervision did so as part of their work assignment. Some full-time and part-time faculty who were not employed by the hospital were paid salaries from the AMH budget. Others were volunteers who lived in Kingston, were Seventh-day Adventists, and had the credentials and expertise to teach or do clinical supervision. Those who were foreign missionaries, such as chairmen of the baccalaureate programme and physicians, were paid by the General Conference of Seventh-day Adventists, the Inter-American Division, or the West Indies Union Conference. WIC provided faculty to teach some of the non-nursing courses at the hospital campus. Likewise, local pastors employed by the East Jamaica Conference and the hospital chaplain taught some of the religion courses.[28] The students paid tuition and general fees to WIC. Costs for housing and food were paid to AMH.[29] In 1971, college expenses for nine months for ladies were J$240.00 for tuition, J$30.00 for fees, J$40.00 for books, J$67.00 for room rent, and J$126.00 for food.[30]

Through the years AMH and clinic had a reputation for providing excellent health care. This resulted in more and more patients seeking care beyond what this Seventh-day Adventist Christian hospital could accommodate. Thus, the AMH Board of Directors realized that it was time to expand the hospital and clinic to help meet the growing health care needs of the Jamaican people.[31] Moreover, the Nursing Council of Jamaica wanted to see the hospital increase its bed capacity from thirty to one hundred beds in order to provide more clinical experiences for the WIC student nurses.[32]

> *Through the years AMH and clinic had a reputation for providing excellent health care.*

On November 28, 1971, there was a ground-breaking ceremony to reconstruct AMH. The Right Honourable Hugh L. Shearer, P.C., Prime Minister of Jamaica, was the main speaker for this event.[33] Dr. Arthur, who was visiting Jamaica as a medical consultant at AMH, gave his full support for this new venture. He was also a major contributor to this initiative.[34] The plans included additional out-patient facilities, consulting and examining rooms, new obstetrical facilities, new operating rooms, and, of course, more hospital beds. The project would take at least five years.[35]

By now the six student nurses were successfully finishing their fall semester of courses. On December 5, 1971, the first WIC Nurses' Capping Ceremony was held in AMH Chapel. Awarding of the cap to a student nurse indicates that she or he has successfully completed a probationary period of schoolwork prior to caring for patients in the hospital.[36] The main address was given by Dr. Standish, president of WIC. He mentioned that the successful nurse "above all else must have a personal acquaintance with the Chief Physician." Standish emphasized that the task of the Christian nurse was not only to relieve the ills of the physical body but to point patients to the One who can heal the spiritual ills as well.[37] The student nurses received their caps from some of the registered general nurses at AMH: Hermina Douglas, Beryl Ellis, Beryl Gilpin, Sonia Henry, Catherine Jamieson, and Janet Jones.[38] Matron Henry led the student nurses in reciting the Florence Nightingale Pledge, and Mrs. Klingbeil lighted the candle in their Florence Nightingale lamps. The students responded by singing, "Take My Hands."[39]

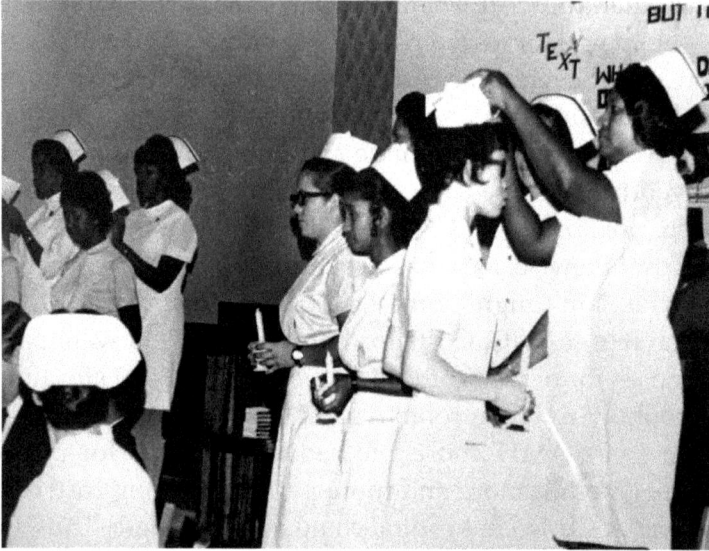

Capping Ceremony for the first class of six West Indies College student nurses. Front row, far left to right: Judith Clayton and Beverley McPherson are not in view, Leonarda Dowdie, Shirlene McLean, Beverley Tai, and Sonia Kennedy being capped by Beryl Gilpin.
Photo: Courtesy of Shirlene McLean.

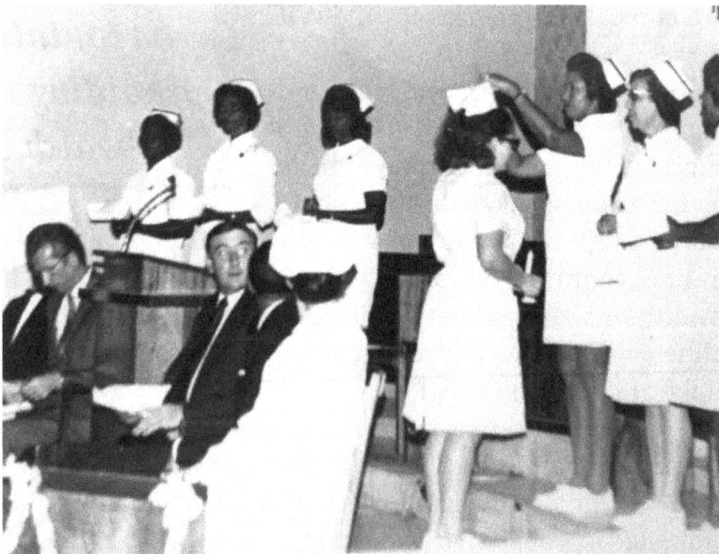

Andrews Memorial Hospital registered general nurses who capped the student nurses.
Back row, left to right: Beryl Ellis, Hermina Douglas, Janet Jones, Sonia Henry capping Shirlene McLean, Catherine Jamieson, and Beryl Gilpin.
Photo: Courtesy of Shirlene McLean.

For spring semester the students continued their studies in Foundations of Nursing, Medical & Surgical Nursing I, Human Relations in Nursing, Human Growth

& Development, a religion course on the Gift of Prophecy, and Health & Physical Education.[40] The course on Health & Physical Education included stationary exercises, walking, running, volleyball, and badminton.[41]

By late spring construction on the nurses' dormitory was nearing completion. On June 4, 1972, it was with much joy that the nurses' dormitory was dedicated and officially opened.[42] The guest speaker was Enid Lawrence, principal tutor, University Hospital of the West Indies School of Nursing, Mona.[43]

Enid Lawrence, principal tutor at University Hospital of the West Indies School of Nursing, giving the main address at the official opening of the new women's dormitory on the Andrews Memorial Hospital campus. Other platform participants, left to right: Mr. Grant, Kingston architect; Mr. Marshalleck, business manager, Andrews Memorial Hospital; Reinhold Klingbeil, pastor and chaplain, Andrews Memorial Hospital campus; Pastor Walters, president, West Indies Union Conference of Seventh-day Adventists; Antoinette Klingbeil, acting chairman, West Indies College Department of Nursing Education; Pastor Roy Williams, treasurer, West Indies Union Conference; and Pastor F. E. White, president, East Jamaica Conference. Dr. Colin Standish, president of West Indies College, and Dr. Herbert Holness, medical director of Andrews Memorial Hospital, are seated behind Mrs. Lawrence but not in view.
Photo: Courtesy of Andrews Memorial Hospital and Alton B. Marshalleck, former business manager, who provided a print of the photograph. Source unknown.

The one-story building accommodated eighteen student nurses, had a dean's apartment, and an assembly room for one hundred individuals.[44] The dormitory also had a washing machine so the students no longer did their laundry by hand. However, there was no clothes dryer, so they still had to hang their laundry on clothes lines to dry in the Jamaican sun and breezes.[45]

The new women's dormitory on the Andrews Memorial Hospital campus.
Photo: Courtesy of Andrews Memorial Hospital and Alton B. Marshalleck, former business manager,
who provided a print of the photograph. Source unknown.

During the summer of 1972, the student nurses took non-nursing courses and obtained clinical experiences at the AMH campus.[46] Upon successful completion of the sophomore year, each student received a royal blue velvet stripe for the left corner of her cap.[47]

On June 30, 1972, Mrs. Klingbeil sent a letter to Enid Lawrence that outlined proposed dates for the WIC student nurses to obtain clinical experiences at University Hospital of the West Indies their junior year. Lawrence responded on July 12, 1972, that the dates would be confirmed later by Matron Lois Dujon. Lawrence also commented that many of the staff at University Hospital of the West Indies School of Nursing expressed their regrets that Klingbeil would not be in Jamaica much longer. Lawrence ended her letter by saying, "Despite the many 'hazards,' we achieved our objectives, due to a great deal of determination."[48] She was referring to the fact that the WIC student nurses would now have access to clinical experiences that were not available at AMH. Thus, the programme would continue to move forward.

On August 15, 1972, Reinhold and Antoinette Klingbeil returned to California.[49] They gave unsparingly of themselves to advance the development of Seventh-day Adventist nursing education in Jamaica and to meet the spiritual needs of those living on this Caribbean Island.

Chapter 10

Antoinette Morrell Klingbeil

Antoinette Klingbeil, Acting Chairman
West Indies College Department of Nursing Education
1971 to 1972
Photo: Courtesy of Northern Caribbean University.

Antoinette Morrell was born on May 14, 1914, to Hiram and Sadie Morrell in Portland, Maine. During her childhood years, she was home-schooled by her mother. The family then moved to Massachusetts so that she and her siblings could attend South Lancaster Academy, a Seventh-day Adventist high school. While a student and for a few years after graduation, Morrell worked in the academy's book bindery.[1]

In due time, she headed to California and earned her nurse's diploma in 1941 from the White Memorial Hospital School of Nursing in Los Angeles. The following year she married Reinhold Klingbeil.[2] Later, Antoinette Klingbeil and her husband, an ordained minister in the Seventh-day Adventist denomination, served for nine years as missionaries in the Curacao Mission, Netherlands West Indies. While living on the island of Aruba, Mrs. Klingbeil conducted health education seminars and cared for her husband and their two sons, David and Jonathan.[3]

In 1954, Mrs. Klingbeil earned her BSc degree in nursing education from Washington Missionary College (now Washington Adventist University) in Takoma Park, Maryland.[4] For the next few years she served the church as a pastor's wife in Coudersport, Pennsylvania.[5] Much of her time was spent in counselling those who had a difficult time getting through life. She also had a heart for people who needed a friend. The Klingbeils often invited people into their home, including students.[6] The family then moved to Victorville, California, where Antoinette Klingbeil was employed as a school nurse.[7]

It was 1961 when Antoinette Klingbeil joined the faculty at Loma Linda University (LLU) School of Nursing and taught psychiatric nursing. While teaching, she earned her MSc degree in psychiatric nursing from the University of California, Los Angeles, in 1968.[8] Three years later Mrs. Klingbeil and her husband accepted the call to once again go as missionaries to the Caribbean region. This time it was the island of Jamaica.[9] Although Antoinette Klingbeil was acting chairman of West Indies College Department of Nursing Education for only one year, it was extremely important to her that a solid foundation be laid upon which others could continue building this new baccalaureate programme. She did whatever was necessary to accomplish that goal.[10] Upon returning to California, Mrs. Klingbeil resumed her faculty responsibilities at LLU until 1973.[11]

> *It was extremely important to her that a solid foundation be laid upon which others could continue building this new baccalaureate programme.*

The Klingbeils then moved to Portland, Oregon. She continued to teach psychiatric nursing at the Good Samaritan Hospital School of Nursing until she retired in 1981. Reinhold and Antoinette Klingbeil lived in Paradise, California, during their retirement years.[12]

Graduates from the Class of 1974 remembered Mrs. Klingbeil as "wise," "an effective communicator," "resourceful," "nurturing," and "a strong yet gentle leader." "She was methodical and systematic in her approach." One graduate commented, "She was someone who understood our concerns." Another remarked, "She taught us to set high goals for ourselves and to be accepting of others."[13]

Upon the death of Pastor Klingbeil, Antoinette Klingbeil continued to live in Paradise with her son Jonathan and two grandchildren.[14] After many years of faithful service to the profession of nursing and to her church, Antoinette Morrell Klingbeil died on December 2, 2003.[15]

CHAPTER 11

Courage to Face Perplexities

While Reinhold and Antoinette Klingbeil were preparing to leave Jamaica, a young woman was saying goodbye to family and friends in the Pacific Northwest part of the United States. Karen J. Radke, MSc, RN, was about to begin the adventure of a lifetime as a licensed, Seventh-day Adventist missionary to a small island in the Caribbean Sea. With much anticipation and excitement she boarded a plane that flew to Miami, Florida. After changing planes in Miami, she completed the last leg of her flight arriving in Kingston, Jamaica, on August 11, 1972.[1]

Radke was the second faculty member from Loma Linda University School of Nursing to serve as acting chairman of West Indies College (WIC) Department of Nursing Education and acting director of Andrews Memorial Hospital (AMH) School of Assistant Nursing. She also served on the AMH Board of Directors. Under her leadership, the junior year of the baccalaureate nursing programme was implemented. She recruited additional faculty for the junior year and continued negotiations for clinical experiences in government-operated facilities for the senior year. She taught courses in both nursing programmes.[2]

It was now September 1972. The first batch of six student nurses were starting their junior year. The second batch of eight young ladies arrived on the AMH campus to begin their sophomore year: Christine Barnes, Heather Boyd, Maggie Burrows, Marilyn Clare, Evadne Cox, Doreen Hardware, Rose Henry, and Maxine Smith. Four of these eight students were from Jamaica. Others were from the Bahamas, Bermuda, Guyana, and the Turks and Caicos Islands.[3]

The fourteen students were delightfully surprised to learn that a Volkswagen minivan had just been purchased to transport them to their clinical affiliations. Money for one-half cost of the minivan came from the AMH budget. Payment for the other one-half cost of the minivan came from money earned at the International Food and Health Fair that was held annually by the AMH Auxiliary Association.[4]

When the second class of students arrived, an interesting responsibility immediately faced Miss Radke. The student nurse uniforms purchased the previous year were extremely expensive. Fortunately, Radke found the same fabric in Jamaica and asked Evauldney Maud Dunbar, sister of AMH staff nurse Catherine Jamieson, to be the seamstress. Miss Dunbar graciously agreed, and the students were most grateful for the reduced cost of their uniforms.[5]

Volkswagen minivan with the first class of six student nurses in August 1972. Left to right: Sonia Kennedy, Beverley McPherson, Beverley Tai, Leonarda Dowdie, Shirlene McLean, and Judith Clayton. Photo by Karen J. Radke.

Although there were many demands on the students with their classes and clinical schedule, there were those who needed to work part-time to help defray the cost of their education. AMH administrators and Miss Radke decided that in the first clinical year, the student nurses could work eight hours per week during fall and spring semesters. They were paid forty cents per hour. In the second clinical year, the student nurses could work sixteen hours per week during fall and spring semesters. They were paid fifty cents per hour.[6] Some of the students worked weekends, holidays, and even vacation days. One student was hired as chief resident advisor and assisted the dormitory dean with various responsibilities.[7]

The house on Hope Road that served as the dormitory the previous year was now used for classrooms and offices of the acting chairman, Karen Radke; Edna Ashmeade, RN, a full-time faculty member for the sophomore year; Myrtle Nelson, DipSS,[8] secretary for the nursing programmes; and Alton Marshalleck, hospital business manager.[9]

For the junior year of the programme, courses taught during fall semester included Obstetric Nursing, Medical & Surgical Nursing II, Communicable Disease Nursing, Introduction to the Humanities, and a religion course on The Life & Teachings of Christ I. During spring semester, Medical & Surgical Nursing III as well as The Life & Teachings of Christ II were taught. In addition, the students took Paediatric Nursing, Pharmacology I, and General Psychology.[10]

Myrtle Nelson, secretary, West Indies College Department of Nursing Education.
Photo: Courtesy of Northern Caribbean University.

For the 1972–1973 academic year, nursing care of obstetrical patients was done at AMH and the out-patient clinic. Medical and surgical nursing experiences were obtained at King George V Sanatorium (now National Chest Hospital) and Mona Rehabilitation Centre (now Sir John Golding Rehabilitation Centre) under the clinical supervision of JoAnn Jones, BSc, RN, who was from the United States. She volunteered part-time to supervise the junior class of student nurses during fall and spring semesters while her

JoAnn Jones, clinical instructor for the first class of student nurses in their junior year, 1972–1973.
Left to right: Mrs. Jones, Beverley McPherson, Leonarda Dowdie, Beverley Tai, Sonia Kennedy, and Shirlene McLean. Judith Clayton is hiding behind Beverley McPherson to tease the photographer.
Photo by Karen J. Radke.

husband was supervisor of the clinical laboratory and X-ray departments at AMH. Additional medical, surgical, and paediatric clinical experiences were obtained at University Hospital of the West Indies during the summer session.[11]

The second batch of student nurses had similar courses and clinical experiences in their sophomore year as did the first group of students. However, a course called Introduction to the Profession of Nursing replaced one credit of Health & Physical Education.[12]

Taking a break from their studies. Front row, left to right: Evadne Cox, Beverley Tai, and Beverley McPherson. Middle row, left to right: Maxine Smith, Marilyn Clare, Leonarda Dowdie, Maggie Burrows, Judith Clayton, and Rose Henry. Back row, left to right: Doreen Hardware and Sonia Kennedy. Photo by Karen J. Radke.

Shortly after Radke assumed her responsibilities as acting chairman, some academic issues came to her attention that reflected growing pains of developing a new programme. Due to ongoing changes in nursing education, she requested that Marilyn J. Christian, dean, and some members of the faculty at Loma Linda University School of Nursing serve as external evaluators to determine that the WIC curriculum met requirements for the BSc degree in nursing. Results of the evaluation showed that an additional course, falling under the umbrella of the humanities, needed to be taught. Upon receiving such information, Dr. Hermon L. Douce, academic dean, and the appropriate committee approved this change. The course, Introduction to the Humanities, was immediately implemented to meet liberal arts requirements for a BSc degree.[13]

Dr. Hermon L. Douce, academic dean, West Indies College.
Photo: Courtesy of Northern Caribbean University.

Another issue that faced Radke and the WIC faculty was the fact that some pre-nursing students were failing the natural science courses and could not progress to the clinical part of the program. In due time effective strategies, such as tutorial sessions, were put in place on the Mandeville campus to prevent repeat occurrences of this problem.[14]

There was also an issue that arose relative to a regulation of the Nursing Council of Jamaica which stipulated that the student must be eighteen years of age at commencement of training (clinical phase of the programme or sophomore year of the baccalaureate nursing programme) to be entered upon the index. The index is a record of student nurses who have been approved by the Council to commence nurses' training and is kept on file in the Council's office.[15]

Approximately mid-semester, Julie Symes, registrar for the Nursing Council of Jamaica, notified Miss Radke that Marilyn Clare (name used with permission), who was in the second batch of students, was not yet eighteen years old when she began the clinical phase of the programme. Thus, she could not be entered upon the index. This was due to an oversight on the part of Miss Radke. Because it was mid-semester, Miss Clare was allowed to finish her courses and participate in the Capping Ceremony. She continued to live in the dormitory, worked part-time in non-nursing departments at AMH, and was a part-time student taking only the non-nursing courses during 1973.[16]

Symes was always cordial, patient, and most generous with her time in explaining the regulations of the Nursing Council of Jamaica. Radke immediately notified Dr. Douce of the problem encountered and recommended that a representative from the WIC Department of Nursing Education be a member of the WIC Admissions Committee, which was done.[17] Moreover, a statement was added to the West *Indies College Bulletin 1973–75* that "the student must be at least seventeen (17) years of age at the point of enrolling in this [four-year, baccalaureate nursing] programme."[18]

On January 14, 1973, the WIC Department of Nursing Education held the second Capping Ceremony at AMH Chapel. The address was given by Dr. Harold Bennett, dean of students, WIC. Miss Radke and Edna Ashmeade, who was class sponsor, introduced the Capping Ceremony. AMH registered general nurses and faculty who participated in capping the student nurses were Lucille Bennett, Hermina Douglas, Beryl Ellis, Shirley Gallimore, Mildred Henry, Sonia Henry, Mabel Kerr, and C. Wilson.

Moira Gallant, faculty, was dressed as Florence Nightingale and lighted the candle in each student's Florence Nightingale Lamp. All nurses in the audience stood to recite the

Capping Ceremony for the second class of student nurses in January 1973.
Left to right: Maggie Burrows, Doreen Hardware, Heather Boyd, Rose Henry,
Maxine Smith, Christine Barnes, Evadne Cox, and Marilyn Clare.
Photo: Courtesy of Northern Caribbean University.

Florence Nightingale Pledge.[19] The newly capped student nurses then sang a song of dedication, "If I Can Help Somebody."[20] The prayer of consecration was offered by Dr. Standish, president of WIC.[21]

Shortly thereafter, Dr. Standish accepted an academic position in the United States.[22] Pastor L. Herbert Fletcher, MA, was appointed president of WIC. He had previously served as secretary, Department of Education and Youth and then treasurer for the West Indies Union Conference.[23]

> *She was one of the trailblazers in nursing education and was adamant that general nursing programmes be incorporated with tertiary educational institutions in Jamaica.*

Prominent nurse leaders such as Enid Lawrence, Norma Woodham, Lois Dujon, and Laurice Hunter-Scott continued to support development of the WIC baccalaureate nursing programme. Moreover, Gertrude Hildegarde Swaby expressed her support of the programme.[24] She was one of the trailblazers in nursing education[25] and was adamant that general nursing programmes be incorporated with tertiary educational institutions in Jamaica.[26] Swaby and Radke often discussed the pioneering work that WIC and AMH were doing to develop a non-traditional, unique programme that would be the first of its kind in Jamaica.[27]

Edna Ashmeade, clinical instructor for the second class of student nurses in their sophomore year, 1972–1973. Front row: Evadne Cox. Middle row, left to right: Heather Boyd, Maxine Smith, and Christine Barnes. Back row, left to right: Doreen Hardware, Mrs. Ashmeade, Rose Henry, and Maggie Burrows.
Photo by Karen J. Radke.

In addition to her trailblazing work in nursing education, Swaby was a technical advisor to the Peace Corps, "the preeminent international service organization of the United States"[28] that was established March 1, 1961, during the presidency of John F. Kennedy.[29] At her request, Miss Radke supervised two Peace Corps trainees doing their teaching practicum with the WIC student nurses. After completion of their training, the Peace Corps workers travelled to Africa to fulfil their assignments.[30]

Another interesting opportunity occurred when two baccalaureate student nurses from Loma Linda University chose Jamaica as the country in which to fulfil requirements for an elective course on Intercultural Nursing. Nurse Edna Ashmeade supervised their clinical experiences at AMH. They lived in the nurses' dormitory and participated in cultural, religious, and social activities with the other students. During this time, Terry and Rhonda Griswold were temporary supervisors in the dormitory while Rosella Nesbitt was on a leave of absence. Mr. and Mrs. Griswold were student missionaries from Pacific Union College in California and were teaching at Kingsway High School.[31]

In addition to administrative and teaching responsibilities, Miss Radke provided in-service education on topics such as communication, teaching methods, clinical supervision, and clinical evaluation to the faculty and staff nurses on the AMH campus. She also served as a consultant on educational matters to Enid Lawrence.[32]

During the three years that each batch of student nurses was on the AMH campus in Kingston, similar religious activities occurred as on the Mandeville campus. They attended evening worship in the dormitory, Bible study and church services on Saturday mornings, and Week of Prayer.[33] Isidore Hodge, BTh, was now the hospital chaplain and the pastor of AMH Chapel.[34]

A spiritual emphasis was also conveyed in the classroom and in the hospital. "When Anna Hoehn taught the religion course, Ministry of Healing, she always began class with the song, 'Lord, Lay Some Soul Upon My Heart,' followed by prayer."[35] Likewise, whenever the student nurses were assigned clinical experiences on the morning shift at AMH, they participated in a worship service with the staff. The student nurses also were taught to pray with their patients providing the patient was receptive to such an offer.[36]

Many of the student nurses implemented their own outreach ministries. They sang to the patients at AMH on Friday evenings, the beginning of the Sabbath day. The first batch of students formed a sextet and often provided special music at various churches, especially when Dr. Holness or Alton Marshalleck preached the sermon. They also sang for an evangelistic crusade in Grand Cayman Island. Dr. Edith Marshalleck often played the piano for the sextet. In the second batch of students there were musicians as well—flutist, pianist, and vocalists—who shared their God-given talents in ministry to others. One student in the sophomore group thoughtfully provided spiritual encouragement to her batchmates by placing a verse of scripture or a spiritual poem on each one's pillow.[37]

Social activities were an important part of student life on the AMH campus, particularly because some student nurses felt isolated from happenings on the main campus at Mandeville. Thus, transportation to Mandeville was provided for the student nurses to participate in the annual school picnic with a variety of games at Kirkvine Field, Feast of Lights, the Lyceum Series, senior convocation, and various banquets. Feast of Lights was a delightful, well anticipated annual Christmas program of carols and music featuring all the choirs and soloists on campus plus popular professional guest artists from the Mandeville community. The Lyceum Series consisted of musical and drama events each semester that exposed the students to different cultural and performing arts activities. Programs that were part of the Lyceum Series also served as a special social event. Students would dress up formally and were allowed to attend with a date. When the young man arrived at the women's dormitory to escort his date to the program, the young lady's name would be announced over the PA system, and she would come to the lounge to join her date. It was always a time of excitement.[38]

Nursing faculty and members of AMH Chapel invited students to their homes. There were also picnics as well as outings to the well-known Rockfort Mineral Bath in the eastern part of Kingston. On occasion, faculty and students had Friday or Sabbath evening worship together at the beach in Harbour View or at Hope Botanical Gardens.

An Outing to Hope Botanical Gardens, Kingston. Front row, left to right: Sonia Kennedy, Beverley Tai, Evadne Cox, Christine Barnes, Leonarda Dowdie, and Judith Clayton. Back row, left to right: Doreen Hardware, Rose Henry, Shirlene McLean, Maxine Smith, and Maggie Burrows. Photo by Karen J. Radke.

Hope Botanical Gardens with the Blue Mountains in the background. Photo by Karen J. Radke.

Some students attended the Advent Fellowship Group that met on Friday evenings at University Hospital of the West Indies.[39] The student nurses also participated in the AMH International Food and Health Fair as well as decorating the hospital for Christmas.[40]

As the junior group of six students approached their senior year of college, they expressed to Miss Radke that some of the dormitory rules were too strict, e.g., the hour that lights were to be turned off in their rooms and the time of curfew when dating on weekends. After listening to their concerns, Radke recommended to the WIC administration in May 1973 that the above mentioned dormitory rules be modified on the AMH campus.[41]

For summer session the junior student nurses cared for medical, surgical, and paediatric patients at University Hospital of the West Indies. Their clinical preceptors were University Hospital of the West Indies registered general nurses. They received their

The end of a day after caring for patients at University Hospital of the West Indies, June 1973. Left to right: Leonarda Dowdie, Beverley Tai, Beverley McPherson, Sonia Kennedy, and Judith Clayton. Photo by Rhonda Griswold.

second royal blue velvet stripe for their caps.[42] Some of the sophomore student nurses returned to the Mandeville campus to take required non-nursing courses.[43] Others worked at AMH.[44] They received their first royal blue velvet stripe for their caps.[45]

On June 10, 1973, it was with much joy that Rebecca Gucilatar received her diploma for the master of science degree in nursing, from Loma Linda University.[46] The next day she returned to Jamaica and resumed her responsibilities as chairman of WIC Department of Nursing Education and director of AMH School of Assistant Nursing.[47]

During orientation sessions with Miss Radke, WIC administrators, and AMH administrators, Gucilatar learned that the college, under the leadership of President Fletcher, was now in a position to financially support the baccalaureate nursing programme.[48] Moreover, she learned that for the first time the nursing and non-nursing faculty on the AMH campus would be listed in the *West Indies College Bulletin 1973–1975*.[49]

Another major change that would take place was the involvement of Miss Gucilatar and some of the nursing faculty with responsibilities on the Mandeville campus. Since WIC would be financially responsible for the baccalaureate nursing programme, there would be more interaction between the two campuses. For the first time, WIC administration would include faculty from the Department of Nursing Education on Standing Committees for the 1973–1974 academic year. Gucilatar would serve on the Academic Policies Committee, Admissions Committee, and Curriculum Development Committee; Edna Ashmeade on the Cultural & Social Committee; Norve Manalo on the Faculty Social Activities Committee; Alton Marshalleck on the Finance Committee and Fund Raising Committee; and the Dean of Women, yet to be named, on the Residence Halls Committee.[50]

Rebecca Gucilatar receiving her diploma for a master's degree in nursing from Dr. David J. Bieber, president of Loma Linda University.
Photo: Courtesy of Loma Linda University, Loma Linda, California.

Towards the end of June, Radke completed orientation sessions with Gucilatar. Miss Radke then returned to the United States. She felt most confident that the first two batches of student nurses and those to follow would graduate and see their dreams come true.[51]

On September 26, 1973, Sonia Kennedy, Class of 1974, wrote to Miss Radke, "The recommendations [modification of dormitory rules] were passed. They make us feel more like adults."[52]

Chapter 12

Karen J. Radke

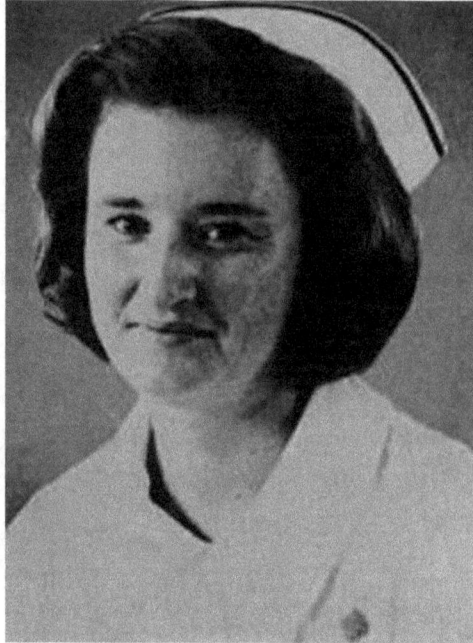

Karen J. Radke, Acting Chairman
West Indies College Department of Nursing Education
1972 to 1973
Photo: Courtesy of Northern Caribbean University.

Karen J. Radke[1] was born on October 20, 1942, in Portland, Oregon, to Edwin and Wilma Radke. She attended Portland Union Academy (now Portland Adventist Academy) then did her freshman year of pre-nursing coursework at Walla Walla College (now Walla Walla University) in the state of Washington. In 1964, Radke earned a BSc degree in nursing from Loma Linda University (LLU), California. For the next two years, she attended Boston University, Massachusetts, and obtained a MSc degree in nursing with a major in biological sciences and a minor in teaching.

Returning to California, Radke worked as a public health nurse for Riverside County Health Department and then as a discharge planner in the Home Care Department at LLU Medical Center. In 1969, she joined the faculty of LLU School of Nursing to teach Community Health Nursing. Later, she was appointed senior year coordinator for the baccalaureate nursing programme. Radke also provided leadership in developing an Intercultural Nursing Elective. Student nurses interested in mission service were assigned to Seventh-day Adventist hospitals and clinics throughout the world as well as Monument Valley Hospital and Clinic located on the Navajo Indian Reservation in the state of Utah, USA.

In May 1972, Marilyn J. Christian, EdDc, dean of LLU School of Nursing, asked Miss Radke if she would accept a call from the General Conference of Seventh-day Adventists to go to Jamaica. After praying about the matter, Radke accepted the appointment. This decision was not surprising. Radke was known as an individual who had an adventuresome spirit, eagerly looked forward to new challenges, and thrived in the academic environment.

After spending a year in Jamaica, Radke returned to the United States and taught Community Health Nursing for Walla Walla College. She then earned a MSc degree as a family nurse clinician (practitioner) from Texas Woman's University, Houston, in 1975. She subsequently joined the faculty at the College of Nursing, University of Tennessee Health Science Center, Memphis, and also practiced in a health clinic located in an underserved community.

In 1983, Radke obtained a PhD in physiology with a minor in pharmacology from Indiana University School of Medicine, Indianapolis. She then returned to the University of Tennessee Health Science Center, Memphis, for a two-year postdoctoral research fellowship in the Department of Physiology, College of Medicine.

After leaving the University of Tennessee, Dr. Radke once again taught students and continued her research on hormones that influence renal function and blood pressure at the University of Rochester School of Nursing and School of Medicine and Dentistry, New York. She presented her research at scientific conferences and published many articles in scholarly journals on physiology and pharmacology. She also published on issues in nursing education.

> *This decision was not surprising. Radke was known as an individual who had an adventuresome spirit, eagerly looked forward to new challenges, and thrived in the academic environment.*

In 1998, Dr. Radke became the associate dean for academic affairs, director of graduate studies, and professor in the School of Nursing, University at Buffalo, The State University of New York. Radke also taught Pharmacokinetics in the School of Nursing and Renal Physiology in the Jacobs School of Medicine and Biomedical Sciences. During her tenure as academic dean, the School of Nursing partnered with H. Lavity Stoutt Community College in Tortola, British Virgin Islands, to assist registered general nurses to obtain their BSc degree in nursing. During her career, she garnered several honours and awards for teaching and research.

Dr. Radke enjoyed doing photography while travelling throughout many parts of the world. She served in various capacities for the Seventh-day Adventist church such as an ordained elder, minister of music, Sabbath School teacher, and chairperson of an Adventist elementary school board. She is retired.

CHAPTER 13

L. Herbert Fletcher

Lee Herbert Fletcher, Jr., President
West Indies College
1973 to 1980
Photo: Courtesy of Northern Caribbean University.

Lee Herbert Fletcher, Jr. was born in Black River, St. Elizabeth, Jamaica, on December 2, 1929, to Lee Herbert, Sr. and Viola Fletcher. His childhood years were spent in Newport, Manchester, and in Highgate, St. Mary, where he attended the local public schools. Fletcher completed his secondary education at New Hope College (now Kingsway High School) in Kingston. He then graduated from West Indian Training College, Mandeville, Jamaica, in 1949. During these years, Fletcher enjoyed the hobby of woodworking and with his father made useable items such as a serving tray inlaid with the map of Jamaica, a highchair for his children, and a mahogany dining room table for the family. Interestingly, Herb Fletcher also enjoyed playing the musical saw.[1,2]

In his junior college years and throughout his life, Fletcher was known for "telling you exactly how he felt. If something made him unhappy, you would know it. After graduation, some months went by before anyone was willing to take the chance of hiring this bright, outspoken young man." Eventually, the president of the West Jamaica Conference hired Fletcher who began his more than forty-five years of service to the church as a teacher and district pastor in Jamaica. These experiences ignited his passion to serve young people and his love for the ministry.[3]

In 1957, Herbert Fletcher married his soul mate, Olive Nation. Soon thereafter, they moved to Washington, D.C., to further their education.[4] He earned a bachelor's degree in religion from Washington Missionary College (now Washington Adventist University) in Takoma Park, Maryland, and in 1960, a master's degree in systematic theology from Andrews University in Berrien Springs, Michigan.[5] During this time, they had a daughter, Barbara, and a son, Lee Herbert, III.[6]

Upon returning to Jamaica in 1960, Pastor Fletcher was director, Department of Education and Youth for the East Jamaica Conference and then for the West Indies Union Conference. Following these positions, he was treasurer for the West Indies Union Conference. In 1973, L. Herbert Fletcher became president of West Indies College (WIC) until 1980.[7]

From 1980 to 1995, Herbert Fletcher was director, Department of Education, Inter-American Division of Seventh-day Adventists, Miami, Florida. He established a graduate extension programme in religion at WIC, and affiliate graduate programmes between the Inter-American Division and Andrews University as well as the Inter-American Division and Loma Linda University. Moreover, he initiated Dominican Adventist University in the Dominican Republic and Venezuelan Adventist University in Venezuela.[8] Fletcher also developed the Inter-American Division Adventist Theological Seminary.[9] In 1984, his book, *Youth Week of Prayer Readings*, was published.[10]

Fletcher was recognized for his many accomplishments. In 1980, he received the Order of Distinction by the Jamaican Government for educating the youth of Jamaica. In 1994, Andrews University bestowed on him the honorary degree, doctor of humane letters, and in 2004, Northern Caribbean University bestowed on him the honorary degree, doctor of divinity.[11] In 2009, the Inter-American Division founded an online distance learning educational institution and named it Herbert Fletcher University in his honour.[12]

After retiring, Herbert Fletcher and his wife continued to live in Miami, Florida. He passed to his rest on November 4, 2009.[13] L. Herbert Fletcher will be remembered for his distinguished leadership and his outstanding contributions to the education of young people.

CHAPTER 14

A Year of Celebrations

In September 1973, the third batch of students began their sophomore year on the AMH campus. They were Joan Collins, Ilene Gentles, Audrey Grant, Elaine Haughton, Joan Haven, Sonia Mahabee, Debra Pully, Elaine Reid, and Gail Simmons. Hermina Douglas, RN, CM, a staff nurse at AMH, was also a student in the Class of 1976 who was taking the necessary WIC courses to obtain her BSc degree in nursing.[1] Seven of the students were from Jamaica, two were from Bermuda, and one was from the Bahamas.[2] As of January 1974, Marilyn Clare, who had been a part-time student during 1973 because of not meeting the age requirement for the programme, was now eligible to be indexed and was a full-time student with the Class of 1976.[3]

There were now twenty-four students on the AMH campus. Twenty-three lived in the dormitory, and Nurse Douglas lived at home.[4] Gladys Brodie ("Aunt Glad") was on call as the dormitory dean in addition to being head of the dietary department at AMH.[5]

Classes continued to be held in the house on Hope Road and in the community rooms at AMH Chapel. However, the basic nursing skills laboratory was now in a building beyond the laundry facilities.[6] The nursing courses and clinical sites remained mostly the same for the sophomore and junior students as in previous years except they did not have clinical experiences at Mona Rehabilitation Centre.[7] The second batch of student nurses, now in their junior year, was the first group from WIC to obtain obstetrical experiences at University Hospital of the West Indies.[8] Changes in non-nursing courses included teachings on the book of Daniel in the Bible instead of Life & Teachings of Christ and a course in Spanish instead of Introduction to the Humanities. Also, Physical Education was no longer taught at the AMH campus.[9] Such changes were due to revision of the curriculum and/or availability of those who had the knowledge to teach specific content.

Under Rebecca Gucilatar's leadership, the senior year of the baccalaureate nursing programme was implemented. The fall semester included courses on Mental Health & Psychiatric Nursing, Public Health Nursing & Community Hygiene, as well as Principles of Administration & Ward Management. Spring semester included courses on Principles of Supervision in Nursing, Professional Adjustment, Methods of Research in Nursing, Principles & Methods of Teaching in Nursing, Anthropology, and the book of Revelation in the Bible.[10]

Clinical experiences for the senior year were obtained at Bellevue Hospital (psychiatric care); Kingston and St. Andrew Corporation health centres, public health nursing units, and school health nursing units; Hyacinth Lightbourne Visiting Nurse Service; health services affiliated with University of the West Indies Department of Social and Preventive Medicine; The St. Andrew Settlement; and Maxfield Park Children's Home.[11] Experiences in nursing administration and ward management were done at AMH and University Hospital of the West Indies.[12]

At the end of fall semester, the third Capping Ceremony occurred. For the first time this event was held in the WIC auditorium on the Mandeville campus rather than in the AMH Chapel.[13] Besides the student nurses who were being capped, the first two batches of student nurses were also in attendance. Others present were church leaders, WIC administrators, WIC nursing faculty, AMH administrators, and AMH staff.[14] Lois Dujon, matron at University Hospital of the West Indies, gave the address and participated in capping the students.

Capping Ceremony for the third class of student nurses being held in the auditorium at West Indies College, Mandeville campus.
Photo by Judith Clayton Gomez.

As the third batch of student nurses (now sophomores) progressed through their academic programme, they, too, were involved in outreach ministries. Some in the group conducted a youth programme in Saint Thomas parish. Others attended Advent Fellowship at the University of the West Indies on Friday evenings. One of the students was a colporteur. When she was twelve years old, she began to sell Seventh-day Adventist Christian books, going from door to door. Through this avenue she earned enough scholarship monies to pay for her high school and college education. While a student nurse she continued to canvas when she had time. Otherwise, whenever she went for a walk, she gave someone a piece of literature or a book. She commented that being a colporteur "was a way of life for me and my seven siblings. We are eternally grateful for the discipline and unshakable foundation instilled in us. To God be the glory!"[15]

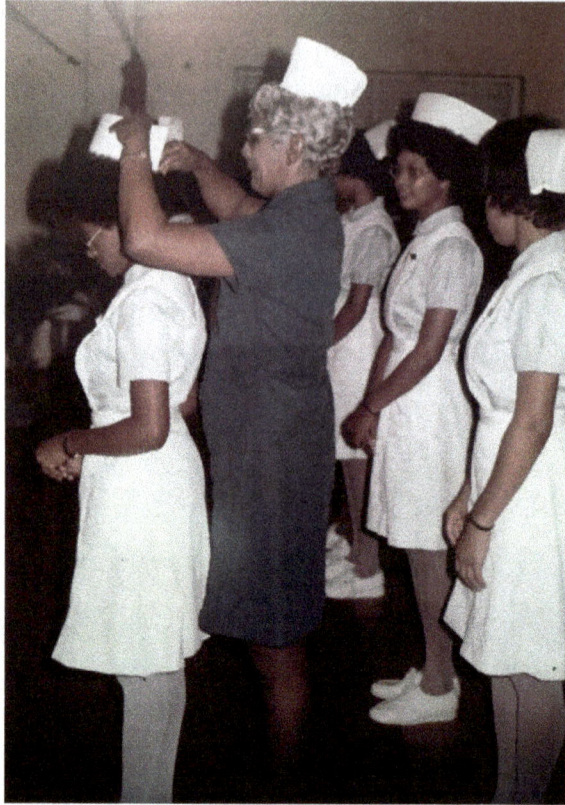

Lois Dujon, administrator of University Hospital of the West Indies School of Nursing, matron of the hospital, and guest speaker, is capping Joan Collins. Batchmates Joan Haven and Gayle Simmons are standing behind them.
Photo: Courtesy of Joan Collins-Ricketts.

The third batch of nine students wearing their nurse's cap. Front row, left to right: Audrey Grant, Elaine Reid, Sonia Mahabee, Elaine Haughton, and Joan Collins. Back row, left to right: Joan Haven, Gail Simmons, Debra Pulley, and Ilene Gentles.
Photo: Courtesy of Joan Collins-Ricketts.

The senial and the dignity

The senior and junior students, likewise, continued to participate in outreach ministries. Some of the student nurses conducted a branch Sabbath School in August Town.[16] Others conducted Sabbath School at AMH Chapel for children from the Maxfield Park Children's Home. Each week Mr. Davidson drove the Volkswagen minivan and transported the children to and from church.[17]

Social activities continued to play an important role on the AMH campus. Faculty invited the student nurses to their homes. Nature walks were done at Castleton Botanical Gardens in St. Mary, and Sabbath evening vespers were done at the beach in Harbour View. The students also participated in church socials.[18]

In January 1974, Enid Lawrence and Norma Woodham visited Loma Linda University in California. Their visit was hosted and sponsored by Marilyn Christian, EdD, dean, Loma Linda University School of Nursing, and Karen Radke, former acting chairman of WIC Department of Nursing Education.[19] The purpose was to determine if Loma Linda University would support WIC in granting the BSc degree in nursing. Lawrence and Woodham met with Dean Christian as well as nursing and medical faculty to discuss Loma Linda University's role in relation to the baccalaureate nursing programme in Jamaica. They also visited clinical facilities and learned more about baccalaureate and graduate education in nursing. Loma Linda University readily gave its support. Upon their return to Jamaica, Lawrence and Woodham gave a report to the Nursing Council of Jamaica. It was an important step towards the Council's recognition of the WIC baccalaureate nursing programme and in preparing for the Council's formal evaluation of the total programme in the future.[20]

> *Being a colporteur "was a way of life for me and my seven siblings. We are eternally grateful for the discipline and unshakable foundation instilled in us. To God be the glory!"*

Laurice Hunter-Scott, principal nursing officer in the Jamaica Ministry of Health, giving main address at the Pinning and Dedication Ceremony for the Class of 1974.
Photo: Courtesy of Sonia Kennedy-Brown.

It was now June 1, 1974. The WIC Department of Nursing Education held the first Pinning and Dedication Ceremony on the Mandeville campus to welcome six young ladies into the nursing profession. The address was given by Laurice Hunter-Scott, principal nursing officer in the Jamaica Ministry of Health.

She also participated in pinning the student nurses along with C. Brooks, RN, Matron Lois Dujon, and L. Grant, RN.[21] Interestingly, a nurse's pin that was designed specifically for WIC had not yet been done. Thus, the SDA (Seventh-day Adventist) Missionary Nurse Pin was used.[22]

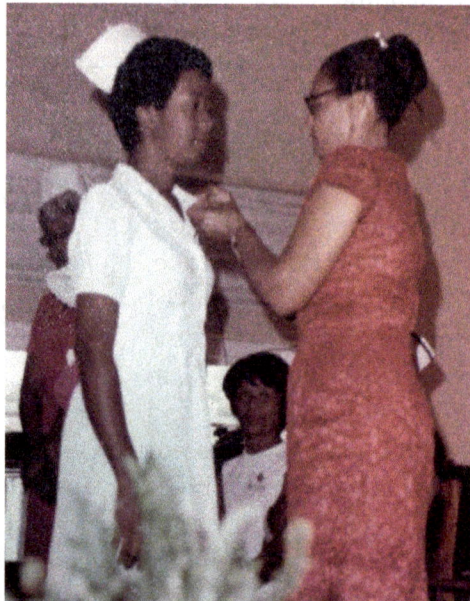

Laurice Hunter-Scott pinning Leonarda Dowdie. Lois Dujon, director of Nursing Service at University Hospital of the West Indies (standing behind Miss Dowdie), and Rebecca Gucilatar-Jakobsen, chairman of West Indies College Department of Nursing Education (seated), observe the pinning.
Photo: Courtesy of Leonarda Dowdie-McKenzie.

The Seventh-day Adventist Missionary Nurse Pin was used as the West Indies College Nurse's Pin in 1974 and for the next few years.
Photo by Shirlene McLean-Henriques.

After each nurse received her pin, there was changing of the stripes.[23] This was a symbolic gesture of becoming a professional nurse. The student nurse's cap with two royal blue velvet stripes was removed. A nurse's cap with a black velvet stripe across the top of the cap was then placed on her head. However, the cap with the black velvet stripe was not worn permanently until she passed the national examination and was registered to practice as a general nurse.[24] Those who participated in changing the caps of the six young ladies were AMH registered general nurses Hermina Douglas, Beryl Ellis, Beryl Gilpin, Sonia Henry, and Catherine Jamieson, as well as former clinical preceptor from the United States, JoAnn Jones.

Sonia Kennedy wearing the professional nurse's cap with a black stripe across the front that is permanently worn after passing the national examination to become a registered general nurse. Photo: Courtesy of Leonarda Dowdie-McKenzie.

The distinguished guest, Laurice Hunter-Scott, was honoured with a gift.

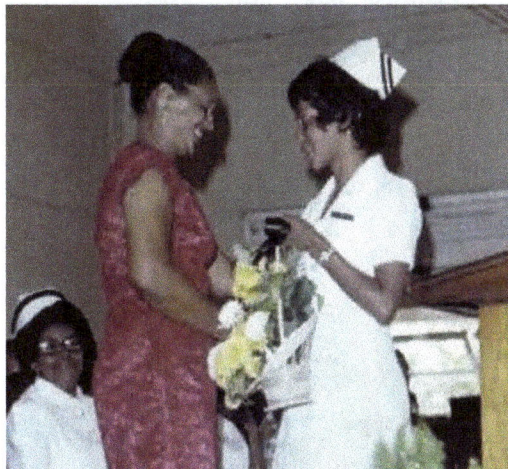

Beverley McPherson presenting a basket of flowers to Laurice Hunter-Scott, guest speaker. Mildred Henry, matron at Andrews Memorial Hospital, is seated behind Mrs. Hunter-Scott. Photo: Courtesy of Beverley McPherson.

Administration of the Pledge was done by Norve Manalo, RN. The Prayer of Dedication was offered by Matron Henry. The Class of 1974 sang, "I May Never Pass This Way Again."[25] In reminiscing about this event, one graduate recently commented to a batchmate, "Pinning Ceremony was a memory you cherish."[26]

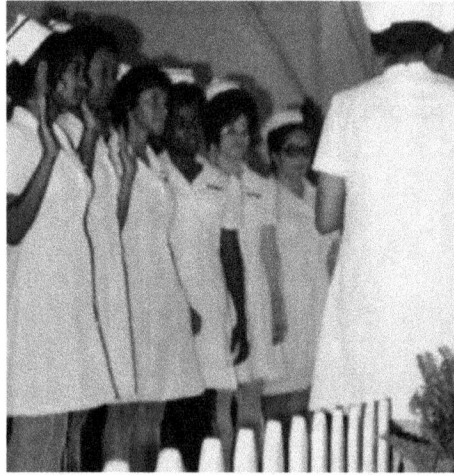

Nurse Manalo leads the graduands in reciting the Florence Nightingale Pledge. Left to right: Beverley Tai, Leonarda Dowdie, Beverley McPherson, Judith Clayton, Sonia Kennedy, and Shirlene McLean. Photo: Courtesy of Sonia Kennedy-Brown.

On Sunday June 2, 1974, the first group of six nurse graduands received their BSc degree in nursing from West Indies College.[27] The Commencement speaker was D. R. B. Grant, MA.[28] Dudley Ransford B. Grant was "an educator who made significant contributions to the development of early childhood education in the region; he was often referred to as the 'Father of Basic Schools' in Jamaica."[29]

Leonarda Dowdie in academic regalia.
Photo: Courtesy of Leonarda Dowdie-McKenzie.

*Time to Celebrate! Left to right: Leonarda Dowdie, Beverley McPherson, Shirlene McLean, Beverley
Tai, Judith Clayton, and Sonia Kennedy.
Photo by Marilyn Clare-Moreau.*

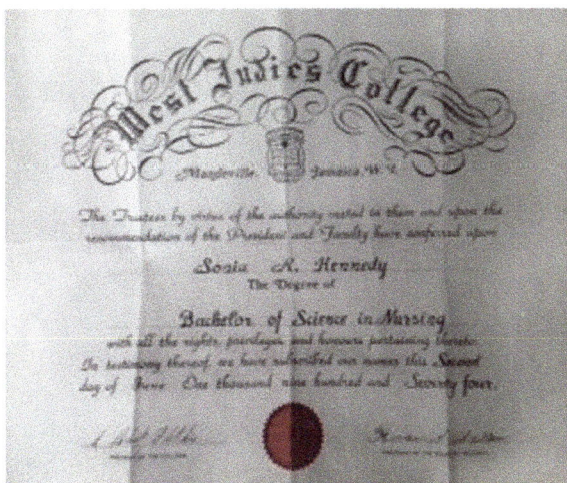

*Sonia Kennedy's diploma for the bachelor of science degree in nursing, West Indies College.
Photo by Sonia Kennedy-Brown.*

For the next three months, the graduates continued to practice under supervision. They also attended review sessions conducted by Matron Henry to prepare for the national examination which was administered in October.[30] Upon passing the examination, each graduate was issued a certificate of registration by the Nursing Council of Jamaica. It stated, in part, "that she is entitled to take and use the title of 'Registered General Nurse.'"[31] The certificate was signed by the chairman of the Council and the registrar. The AMH Board of Directors adjusted the salary scale for this new category of professional nurse—a registered general nurse with a bachelor of science degree in hand![32]

CHAPTER 15

Mildred Richards Henry

Matron Mildred Henry (right) with Nurse C. B. Gayle
Andrews Memorial Hospital
1962 to 1977
Photo by the late Arthur E. Sutton. Courtesy of his daughter,
U.S. Army Brigadier General (Retired) Loree K. Sutton, MD.

Mildred Richards was born on March 4, 1923, to Herbert and Elizabeth Richards (née Angel) in Savanna-la-Mar, Westmoreland Parish, Jamaica. In 1948, Richards earned her nurse's diploma from Andrews Memorial Hospital and Clinic School of Nursing in Kingston as a member of the first class of graduates. After becoming a registered nurse (RN), she attended Victoria Jubilee Lying-In-Hospital School of Midwifery in Kingston and became a certified midwife (CM).[1]

From 1950 to 1953, Mildred Richards was a staff nurse at Kingston Public Hospital. During this time, she married Rupert Henry. For the next four years, Mildred Henry was a staff nurse and midwife at several government hospitals in Jamaica. Mrs. Henry and her husband had three children: Patricia, Rose, and Michael.[2]

In 1957, Mildred Henry, along with her husband, attended Atlantic Union College in Massachusetts. She also worked as a nurse at Branson Hospital in Toronto, Canada. Upon graduating in 1961 with a BSc degree in nursing, she and her husband returned to Jamaica.[31]

In addition to being the matron (director of nursing service) at Andrews Memorial Hospital (AMH), Henry was director of the AMH School of Assistant Nursing until 1969 and continued to teach in the programme until 1977.[4] Mildred Henry was the first Jamaican national to serve in these two leadership positions. She was also a member of the AMH Board of Directors.[5]

Matron Henry was instrumental in fostering the success of the West Indies College (WIC) baccalaureate nursing programme. She arranged for several of the nursing staff at AMH to provide classroom teaching and clinical instruction in their areas of expertise. Mildred Henry was also herself a faculty member in the programme.[6]

Matron Henry was highly regarded by her peers and was a member of the Nursing Council of Jamaica. She was influential in procuring approval from the Council for the education of professional general nurses within a tertiary institution such as WIC.[7]

In 1977, Henry migrated to the United States and continued to work as a nurse educator. She was a member of City Tabernacle of Seventh-day Adventists in New York where she sang in the choir and was a pianist.[8]

Some of the baccalaureate graduates in nursing whom Matron Henry taught remembered her as "inspiring," "approachable," "encouraging," and "fair." "She wore her nurse's uniform with pride." "She was one who stuck to the rules." "She used real life case studies to encourage critical thinking." One graduate recalled, "When she told us a story from her experiences, she always started with and had us repeat, 'I will hold in confidence all personal matters committed to my keeping.'"[9] This was a phrase from the original Florence Nightingale pledge.[10] Another graduate commented, "She had a great sense of humour and a real raucous laugh. I can just hear her now."[11]

Mrs. Henry was still working when she unfortunately became ill in June 2008 and moved to Bridgetown, Barbados, to be with her daughter, Patricia, and son-in-law. She died June 6, 2009. At Matron Henry's request, she was dressed in a full nurse's uniform for her funeral.[12] Mildred Richards Henry will always be known as a faithful, industrious, and committed Seventh-day Adventist nurse leader and educator.

Chapter 16

Growing with the Challenges

It was now September 1974 and the beginning of another academic year. The second batch of student nurses (now juniors) had taken care of patients during the summer at University Hospital of the West Indies and received the second blue stripe for their caps.[1] The third batch of student nurses completed their sophomore year and received the first blue stripe for their caps.[2]

During 1974, a second floor was added to the women's dormitory.[3] A new library was located on the second floor, and classes were held there as well. Marcheta Holness was the librarian. Rebecca Gucilatar's office was relocated from the house on Hope Road to the second floor of the women's dormitory.[4] Gretel Ashley was appointed Dean of Women.[5]

The women's dormitory with a new second floor that had a library, an office for Miss Gucilatar, classrooms, and additional dormitory rooms for the student nurses.
Photo by Sonia Kennedy-Brown.

Marcheta Holness, librarian on the Andrews Memorial Hospital campus.
Photo: Courtesy of Northern Caribbean University.

Once again, the demands on Gucilatar's time increased remarkably. The fourth batch of ten student nurses began their clinical phase of the baccalaureate programme. There were nine young ladies: Dahana Baxter, Miriam Daley, Charmaine Morris, Tamari Nkiriyehe, Pauline Powell, Olivette Simmonds, Verna Spence, Claudette Wint, and Allison Young. The first young man in the programme was Charles Williams.[6] Thus, the house on Hope Road that had been used for offices and classrooms became the men's dormitory.[7] Unfortunately, information was not available regarding their Capping Ceremony.

There were now twenty-eight WIC student nurses, including staff nurse Hermina Douglas, on the AMH campus. Many of the same faculty, clinical instructors, and AMH staff nurses continued to teach in the programme as in the previous year. In addition, four individuals were recruited to teach nursing courses and/or do clinical supervision: Gretel Ashley, BSc, RN; Judith Clayton, BSc, RN; Leonarda Dowdie, BSc, RN; and T. Palima, BSc, RN, CM.[8]

It was also in September that Mazie Herin, who had been a consultant to Miss Gucilatar during development of the WIC baccalaureate nursing programme, visited the Department of Nursing Education. She outlined fifteen points relative to the organization and operation of a college-controlled programme in nursing and requested that the college administration, faculty, and nursing service at AMH give study to the document. Herin also noted in her report that Gucilatar had completed a questionnaire in which she described the baccalaureate programme as required by the Nursing Council of Jamaica Board of Review.[9]

Late in 1974, the Nursing Council of Jamaica Review Board did an on-site visit and evaluated the WIC Department of Nursing Education. It was good news that the curriculum for the WIC Department of Nursing Education was approved. On the other hand, it was noted that new graduates of the WIC programme did not have the experiences required by the Nursing Council of Jamaica to be teaching. It was also noted that the bed capacity at AMH was inadequate. With every bed occupied the number of in-patients was not enough for the learning and practice of nursing care by students in two different programmes—WIC baccalaureate nursing programme and AMH School of Assistant Nursing.[10]

Throughout the early years of the programme, Chairmen Gucilatar, Klingbeil, and Radke made every effort to recruit faculty who had the academic qualifications and clinical experiences to participate in a baccalaureate nursing programme. However, availability of additional faculty and budget restraints were constant issues.[11] In response to the other concern of the Council, parts of AMH were reconfigured throughout 1975 to increase the bed capacity from 30 to 40.[12] However, the resources at AMH were still too limited for the operation of two different nursing programmes.[13] In 1978, the decision would be made to close the AMH School of Assistant Nursing so that AMH resources could more fully support the WIC baccalaureate nursing programme.[14]

On February 11, 1975, Miss Gucilatar wrote a letter to Enid Lawrence, who was now director of Nursing Education, University Hospital of the West Indies School of Nursing, regarding a contract for WIC student nurses to use their clinical facilities. Copies of the contract were provided to Lawrence, Lois Dujon, who was now director of nursing service, and the hospital administrator (name unknown) for their viewing and suggestions.[15] The contract between the two institutions was signed.[16]

In 1978, the decision would be made to close the AMH School of Assistant Nursing so that AMH resources could more fully support the WIC baccalaureate nursing programme.

Certainly the challenges of developing a new programme in Jamaica brought its rewards, but living in Jamaica also brought other rewards. In 1974, Gucilatar met Kresten Jakobsen, who worked for the United Nations in Jamaica. They were married on March 30, 1975.[17]

The time finally arrived for another commencement weekend and more celebrations. On May 31, 1975, the Pinning and Dedication Ceremony was held in the WIC auditorium for the second group of student nurses. The address was given by Enid Lawrence. The pinning was done by registered general nurses C. Brooks, Lois Dujon, E. Newell, and Norma Woodham. The changing of stripes was done by AMH registered general nurses and WIC nursing faculty: Lucille Bennett, M. Carr, Beryl Ellis, Moira Gallant, Mildred Henry, T. Palima, and C. Wilson. Matron Henry administered the pledge, and Moira Gallant offered the prayer of dedication. The Class of 1975 sang, "Help Somebody Today."[18, 19]

On June 1, 1975, the second class of seven graduands received their BSc degree in nursing from WIC. The commencement address was given by Esther Harriott Ottley, PhD.[20] She was a long-time educator in the Department of Mathematics at Howard University in Washington, D.C.[21] Unfortunately, photographs of the Pinning and Dedication Ceremony and nurse graduates were not available. During the summer, the graduates did more clinical practice under supervision and prepared for the national examination to become a registered general nurse. Matron Henry, Nurse Edna Ashmeade, and Nurse Sonia Henry conducted the review sessions.[22]

CHAPTER 17
Alton B. Marshalleck

Alton Brandis Marshalleck, Business Manager
Andrews Memorial Hospital
1970 to 1975 and 1979 to 1985
Photo: Courtesy of Northern Caribbean University.

Alton Brandis Marshalleck[1] was born on December 5, 1934, in Kingston, Jamaica, to Rudolph P. and Williamheina L. Marshalleck (née James). He completed his secondary education at Kingsway High School and in 1958 obtained a diploma in business administration from West Indian Training College, Mandeville, Jamaica. He then worked as an accountant for the West Jamaica Conference of Seventh-day Adventists.

In pursuit of further education, Marshalleck graduated in 1962 with an AASc degree in business administration from Rochester Institute of Technology in New York. The following year he earned a BSc degree in accounting from Atlantic Union College in Massachusetts. In 1964, Alton Marshalleck returned home to Jamaica and married Edith G. Mullings. They had two children, Sheryl and Hans.

Committed to the work of the Seventh-day Adventist church, Marshalleck was an accountant for the West Indies Union Conference, acting treasurer for the Bahamas Mission, treasurer for the West Jamaica Conference, and secretary-treasurer of the East Jamaica Conference. From 1970 to 1975, he served as business manager at Andrews Memorial Hospital (AMH).

In 1975, Marshalleck enrolled at Andrews University in Michigan. He earned a master of arts degree in teaching and a master's degree in business administration. His wife Edith obtained a master's degree in education and later a doctoral degree in education.

Returning to Jamaica in 1979, Marshalleck was the administrator at AMH. During his twelve years as business manager/administrator, he was actively involved with the first phase of transforming the hospital into a modern hospital complex. The project involved adding doctors' offices and a surgical recovery room, refurbishing the paediatrics department, relocating the new pharmacy, reorganizing medical records, building a nurses' dormitory, expansion of housing for personnel, and purchasing two adjacent properties.

In 1985, Marshalleck left the arena of hospital administration and later continued his career in academia. For a short period he was vice-president of development at West Indies College (WIC) and for several years was a faculty member in the Department of Business Administration and Economics.

While living primarily in Jamaica, Marshalleck served the church for more than thirty-three years. He was a board member of the conferences, mission, hospital, and college in which he served. He was also a member of the Blue Cross of Jamaica Board.

In 1997, Alton Marshalleck retired from WIC, and Dr. Edith Marshalleck retired from being permanent secretary, Ministry of the Public Service, Jamaica. They then migrated to Orlando, Florida. Mr. Marshalleck continues to faithfully serve the Lord. He is an elder at the North Orlando Seventh-day Adventist Church and has assisted the treasurer for over twelve years.

Alton Brandis Marshalleck is lauded for his unwavering commitment to improve health care services at AMH. He is also commended for supporting development and growth of the WIC baccalaureate nursing programme.

CHAPTER 18

Into the Future with Confidence

Once again September arrived. The fifth batch of eight student nurses began their sophomore year: Gloria Barnes, Beverley Corrodus, Barbara deRoux, Gaynell Ford, Tabitha Ochoa, Yvette Reynolds, Olivene Rochester, and Nerissa Sterling. There were now twenty-nine WIC student nurses on the Andrews Memorial Hospital (AMH) campus.[1]

On November 16, 1975, a Capping and Candle-Lighting Ceremony for the fifth class was held in the WIC Auditorium in Mandeville. The address was given by Dr. Mary J. Seivwright, director, Advanced Education Unit, University of the West Indies, Mona. The students were capped by faculty and AMH registered general nurses: F. Amritt, Gretel Ashley, Judith Clayton, Rebecca Gucilatar-Jakobsen, Mildred Henry, Catherine Jamieson, Sonia Kennedy, Leonarda Dowdie-McKenzie, and Shirley Purchas. Nurse Hermina Douglas was dressed as Florence Nightingale and lighted the candle in each student's Florence Nightingale lamp. Matron Henry administered the Florence Nightingale Pledge, and Nurse Jamieson offered the prayer of dedication. The class song was, "If Any Little Word of Mine."[2] Unfortunately, photographs of the ceremony were not available.

In her final year as chairman from 1975–1976, Mrs. Gucilatar-Jakobsen faced many issues. Student enrolment in the WIC nursing programme continued to increase. In addition, the Nursing Council of Jamaica gave its approval to accept thirty freshmen students who were enrolled in the pre-nursing curriculum on the Mandeville campus. However, there was no guarantee that the provisional approval of the schema would be extended to students who might be admitted as freshmen in September 1976.[3]

Ongoing dialogue ensued among Hiram Walters, president of the West Indies Union Conference of Seventh-day Adventists; Herbert Fletcher, president of WIC; AMH Board of Directors; and the Nursing Council of Jamaica regarding the operation of WIC Department of Nursing Education.[4] Moreover, Gucilatar-Jakobsen continued to provide information about the baccalaureate nursing programme as requested by Julie Symes, registrar of the Council. On April 21, 1976, Walters wrote a letter to Mrs. Gucilatar-Jakobsen expressing "sincere hope and trust that the information supplied will make some difference in regard to the decisions to be made by the Nursing Council toward continuing the programme." President Walters thanked Gucilatar-Jakobsen for the great work that she was doing.[5]

By June 1976, it was time for WIC Department of Nursing Education to renew its written contract with University Hospital of the West Indies Department of Nursing Service for WIC student nurses to obtain clinical experiences there. Written contracts based on previous groundwork also needed to be done with National Chest Hospital and Bellevue Hospital for the first time. Likewise, verbal arrangements with the Kingston and St. Andrew Corporation for public health and school health nursing experiences as well as The St. Andrew Settlement and the University of the West Indies Department of Social and Preventive Medicine for public health nursing experiences needed to be transformed into written contracts.[6]

Senior student nurses leaving Bellevue Hospital after a morning of clinical practice.
Front row, left to right: Marilyn Clare, Joan Haven, and Audrey Grant.
Back row, left to right: Debra Pully, Ilene Gentles, and Gail Simmons.
Photo by Judith Clayton Gomez.

There were also many social agencies that were accessed based on verbal arrangements. For example, there was Operation Friendship, Jamaica National Children's Home, Backyard Nurseries for Low-income Groups, Home for the Aged, and Salvation Army for the Blind.[7]

A major issue facing WIC administration was to hire full-time, academically-qualified faculty with a MSc degree in nursing and experiences in various clinical nursing specialties. It was absolutely essential to decrease reliance on short-term foreign missionaries to serve as chairmen and on AMH staff nurses to teach courses and be clinical preceptors in order to stabilize the baccalaureate nursing programme. Looking to the future and the trend in nursing education, it was imperative that future chairmen have a PhD in nursing or a relevant discipline. It was also desirable that the chairmen and faculty be of Jamaican heritage.[8, 9]

Other issues facing WIC administration were to: (1) hire a full-time librarian at the AMH campus; (2) increase facilities for classrooms, faculty offices, an up-to-date nursing skills laboratory, a conference room, and storage space; (3) increase teaching aids such as audio-visual media and library resources; and (4) address dormitory needs such as an office for the residence hall dean, full-time janitor, dating parlour, chairs for the worship room, and a spacious social hall.[10]

During spring semester, Mrs. Gucilatar-Jakobsen continued to revise the curriculum that was published in the *West Indies College Bulletin: 1976–1978*. Principles of Education, Algebra, and Zoology were no longer required. This made it possible to increase the number of credits for Anatomy and Physiology, Foundations of Nursing, and Medical-Surgical Nursing. Principles of Psychology replaced General Psychology, and Anthropology replaced Introduction to Sociology.[11, 12]

> *It was absolutely essential to decrease reliance on short-term foreign missionaries to serve as chairmen and on AMH staff nurses to teach courses and be clinical preceptors in order to stabilize the baccalaureate nursing programme.*

Towards the end of spring semester Audrey Grant, a senior student nurse, represented WIC in a competition sponsored by The Nursing Students' Association of Jamaica. A senior student from each school of nursing in Jamaica answered multiple questions in three different sessions before a panel of judges.[13] Grant won the coveted title, "The Top Student Nurse of the Year."[14]

On June 4, 1976, WIC Commencement Weekend began. Kenneth G. Vaz, former president of WIC, gave the homily for the Friday night Consecration Service. One of the nurse graduands recalled that he said, "'World, here I come with my BA. And the world will say, now sit down and let me teach you the rest of the alphabet.'"[15]

The following day, the third Pinning and Dedication Ceremony was held at WIC. Lois Dujon, RN, CM, director of the Department of Nursing Service at University Hospital of the West Indies, gave the address. For the first time, parents participated in the Pinning Ceremony.

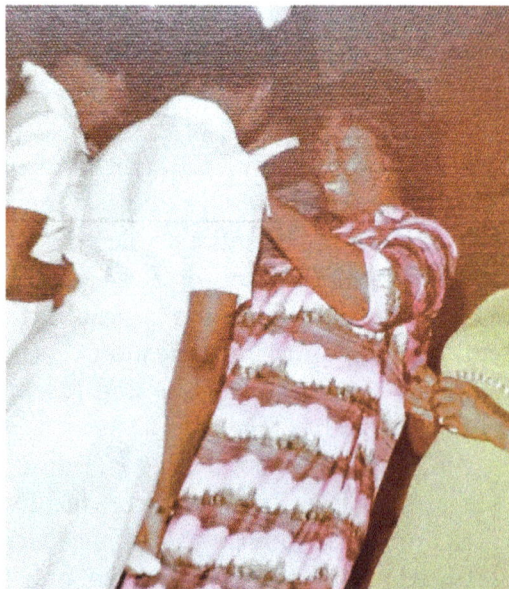

Joan Collins being pinned by her mother, Mrs. Madge Gregory.
Photo: Courtesy of Joan Collins-Ricketts.

The Changing of Stripes was done by several of the AMH registered general nurses: Gretel Ashley, Lucille Bennett, Hermina Douglas, Beryl Ellis, Jean Fletcher, Mildred Henry, Sonia Henry, O. McLean, and Beverley McPherson. Administration of the Pledge was conducted by Bernice F. Buchanan, PhD, RN. The Prayer of Dedication was given by Pastor Isidore Hodge. The Class of 1976 sang "Through It All."[16]

The Class of 1976 with the Seventh-day Adventist Missionary Nurse Pin above each one's name.
Left to right: Joan Haven, Gail Simmons, Elaine Reid, Audrey Grant, Ilene Gentles, Marilyn Clare,
Debra Pulley, Joan Collins, and Elaine Haughton.
Photo: Courtesy of Ilene ("Irene") Gentles-Patrick.

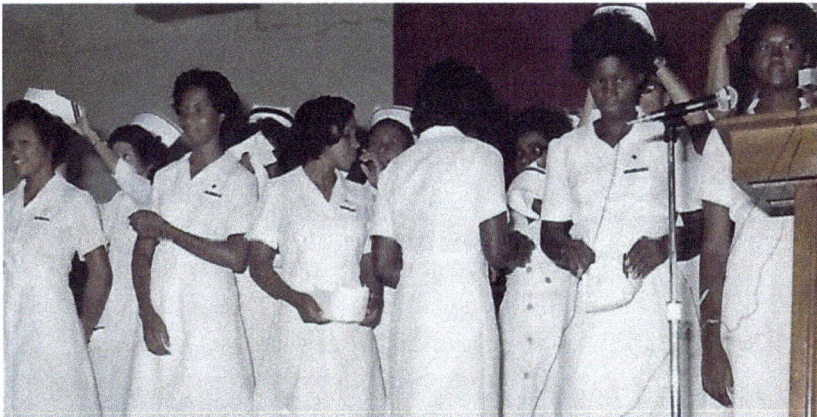

The Changing of Stripes. A registered general nurse removes the student nurse's cap with the two
blue stripes and places a professional nurse's cap with a black stripe on the student's head during
the Pinning and Dedication Ceremony. The professional nurse's cap is permanently worn only after
passing the national examination to become a registered general nurse.
Front row, left to right: some members of the Class of 1976 are Joan Haven, Gayle Simmons,
Elaine Reid, Audrey Grant facing backwards, Ilene Gentles, and Marilyn Clare.
Back row, left to right: registered general nurses are Beverley McPherson, Mildred Henry (hidden),
Beryl Gilpin, Jean Fletcher, and unidentified gentleman (hidden).

Photo: Courtesy of Ilene ("Irene") Gentles-Patrick.

On June 6, 1976, nine nurse graduands received their BSc degree in nursing from WIC. Dr. Walter Douglas, professor of Church History at Andrews University in Berrien Springs, Michigan, gave the Commencement address.[17]

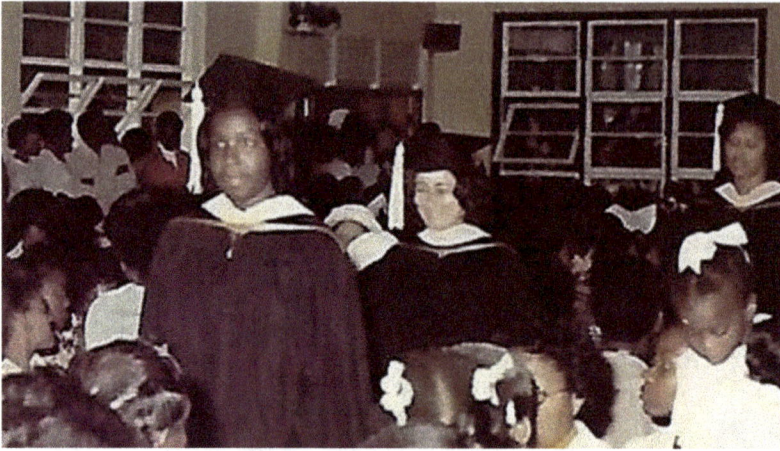

Graduands walking into the auditorium at West Indies College, Mandeville campus, to receive their diplomas for a bachelor of science degree in nursing: Audrey Grant, Elaine Haughton, and Joan Haven. Photo: Courtesy of Ilene ("Irene") Gentles-Patrick.

In July, Marilyn Clare, who had just graduated, was sent as a representative from WIC to the Caribbean Nurses' Association Conference in Barbados, West Indies. While a student, she was a member of The Nursing Students' Association of Jamaica and helped with formally organizing the association.[18]

During the summer of 1976, the new graduates did clinical practice at University Hospital of the West Indies under the supervision of Nurse Edna Ashmeade.[19] They also attended review sessions conducted by Matron Henry and Nurse Lucille Bennett to prepare for the national examination to become registered general nurses.[20]

> *West Indies College Department of Nursing Education had a beginning that was embedded with an abundance of faith, courage to face perplexities, and perseverance to boldly move forward.*

That same summer Rebecca Gucilatar-Jakobsen and her husband left Jamaica to reside in California.[21] She had spent five years of her life to design, develop, and implement the first baccalaureate nursing programme in Jamaica.[22] Much had been accomplished due to her leadership, persistence, and seemingly unlimited energy to make the programme a success. Twenty-three young ladies were now WIC graduates with a BSc degree in nursing.

West Indies College Department of Nursing Education had a beginning that was embedded with an abundance of faith, courage to face perplexities, and perseverance to boldly move forward. Such an initiative seemed to be improbable, if not impossible. It was only through the power and providences of God that doors opened time and again. The right people at the right time were there when needed. Prayers for divine wisdom ascended heavenward, and each crisis was met with a faithful God answering the prayers of His dependent children with their human inadequacies. Miracles of divine intervention happened time and again. And so it was that a vision became reality.

Chapter 19

Many Roads Travelled Serving God and Humanity

After the graduates received their bachelor of science degree in nursing from West Indies College (WIC), their next step was to pass the national examination to become registered general nurses. Once this was achieved, they were prepared to launch their careers as professional nurses. No matter how daunting the challenges might be, they were eager to face them with the energy and enthusiasm characteristic of young adults who feel ready to leave the safety of a college environment and make their mark in the world.

Those who were involved in teaching and mentoring the student nurses instilled in them certain values that are hallmarks of successful living. First and foremost, keep Christ central in all that you do. Be dedicated to your chosen profession. Remember, learning is a lifetime adventure. Be passionate about service to others. Take time for family and friends. Have fun along the way.

From August 2014 to June 2019, seventeen graduates who represent the Classes of 1974, 1975, and 1976 were interviewed by one of the authors.[1] The purpose of these interactions was to learn about each one's journey beyond graduation.

Nursing Careers

Twelve of the graduates began their careers as staff nurses. Nine of them provided patient care on a hospital medical and/or surgical unit, one on an obstetrical unit, one on a sub-acute gerontology unit, and one in a long-term care facility. Five of these nine graduates were staff nurses at Andrews Memorial Hospital (AMH). Three graduates began their careers by teaching at AMH School of Assistant Nursing; one of them was also the assistant director. Two graduates began their careers by teaching for WIC Department of Nursing Education.

Through the years, many of the graduates ventured into different areas of nursing practice that included caring for all ages of people from the newborn to the elderly. Most of them at some point cared for patients in various hospitals. Others provided nursing care in rehabilitation facilities, patients' homes, schools, industries, primary care clinics, or correctional facilities. Two of the graduates were travel nurses in the United States.

Several of the graduates advanced to positions of leadership in hospitals such as head nurse, nursing supervisor, director of nursing service, in-service coordinator, or case manager. Two of the graduates became administrators of home health agencies, and one graduate became director of health services at WIC. One graduate was a provider relations officer for a major health insurance company. Another graduate was deputy chief executive officer of the health services authority for one of the Caribbean Islands as well as a regional director for ADRA (Adventist Development and Relief Agency). One graduate along with her family spent seven years in the mission field in Nairobi, Kenya, where she served as the Rural Health Department Purchasing Coordinator for medical supplies and medications. She also served as liaison with ADRA Kenya to the World Food Organization and USAID.

Nine of the graduates who began their careers in nursing practice became involved in education and/or administration. One graduate was principal tutor for a school of practical nursing in the Caribbean. The other eight graduates were faculty at various colleges or universities. Three graduates taught nursing for WIC. Through the years one graduate from the Class of 1974 and two graduates from the Class of 1975 were appointed to serve as director of WIC Department of Nursing Education. One graduate was chairperson for a collegiate school of nursing and allied health professions in the Bahamas. Another graduate was associate vice-president for student services at a college in the USA.

Advanced Education

It is without question that these graduates were highly motivated to obtain further education in their chosen areas of nursing. Many of the graduates became certified in a specialty area of nursing practice after earning the baccalaureate degree in nursing. For example, two graduates became certified midwives.

Fifteen graduates earned a master's degree. One specialized in mental health and psychiatric nursing, one in marriage and family therapy, seven in public health, three in nursing education, one in educational psychology, one in management of health care facilities, and one in administration.

Some of the graduates also continued with post-master's education. One earned a post-master's certificate as a family nurse practitioner, and another graduate did a post-master's programme studying informatics.

Three of the graduates earned a second master's degree. One became a family nurse practitioner with further study in adolescent medicine. The other obtained a master's degree in health sciences with a major in substance abuse counselling. Another graduate earned a master's degree in public health.

Two graduates earned a doctoral degree. One obtained a PhD in family therapy, and another graduate earned a DNP, doctoral degree in nursing practice. She commented, "It's important to keep on learning."

Honours and Awards

With such a stellar group of graduates who had accomplished so much in their careers, it is not surprising that many were recognized for their excellence in nursing practice and distinguished service to the profession of nursing. Other graduates received awards for outstanding contributions as nurse educators. Three graduates were recognized as outstanding alumna from their respective institutions of higher learning, and one graduate was awarded the WIC President's Medallion. Moreover, some were recognized for service to their communities as well as improving health care in the Caribbean region and other parts of the world. One graduate was a recipient of the Queen's Certificate and Badge of Honour for her gallant work with persons with AIDS. Accolades were given to these graduates, not only by professional organizations, educational institutions, and governments, but by honour societies and corporations as well.

Publications

One graduate published her autobiography. She also wrote pieces about her life with a spiritual application that were included in three books of women's devotionals. Others published articles in their local and regional Seventh-day Adventist church papers or magazines, local newspapers, and professional journals. Some were involved in writing guidelines and policies for professional practice. Another participated in developing a government-level strategic plan for healthy living on one of the Caribbean Islands. Interestingly, one of the graduates developed a board game to teach teenagers about HIV, and another graduate developed a board game called "Bible Appetizer."

Church Involvement

The degree to which these graduates have been involved in the Seventh-day Adventist church is extensive. Almost every position in the local church has been held by at least one of the graduates, including ordained head elder. Most of the graduates have held multiple church positions and, in some instances, have been members of their church board. Service to the church has been without monetary remuneration. Most continue to hold positions in the Seventh-day Adventist church to this day.

Community Service

Loving, voluntary service to others has always been a mission of the Seventh-day Adventist denomination. These graduates of WIC Department of Nursing Education wholeheartedly embrace such a philosophy. One founded an Alzheimer's support group, another founded a women's crisis centre, while yet another graduate founded a non-profit organization to provide community services to disenfranchised individuals. One graduate prepares meals for the homeless as well as those who are handicapped, elderly, and ill but living in their homes. Another delivers meals on wheels. Several graduates organize or participate in health fairs, teach breast cancer awareness, and cardio-pulmonary resuscitation. Others give freely of their time to provide health care at established community clinics, a rape crisis centre, or during mission trips. One graduate voluntarily gives Bible studies at the Department of Corrections, and another conducts church-based seminars on relationship issues.

One graduate, elected by her local national nurses' association, voluntarily coordinated and conducted seminars and workshops on a variety of topics. She also chaired the Nursing Council, a government-appointed position, on a voluntary basis. Another graduate volunteered her time as chief nursing officer for the Red Cross and executive director for the Aids Foundation on one of the Caribbean Islands. She also served on the WIC Board of Governors. One graduate did voluntary service by painting the stage sets for her local community theatre.

> *With such a stellar group of graduates who had accomplished so much in their careers, it is not surprising that many were recognized for their excellence in nursing practice and distinguished service to the profession of nursing.*

Finally, the academic community is always appreciative of their alumni giving financial support to their alma mater. One of the graduates established the Pioneer Scholarship Fund at WIC Department of Nursing Education to annually assist one senior student nurse with his or her tuition. This commitment has now been embraced by the entire Pioneer Class of 1974.

Family

As often happens, many of the graduates met their husbands prior to or during their time at WIC. Others met their husbands later in life. Thirteen of the seventeen graduates married. Twelve of those who married have children, and some have grandchildren. Although four are now widows and one is divorced, they continue to enjoy life to the fullest as do the other graduates.

Graduates' Personal Comments

Some of the graduates made unsolicited comments regarding their time spent at WIC. One remarked, "I was baptized by Elder H. E. Nembhard after listening to him explain Bible principles in his class, Christian Education. My first year at WIC was one of the most transforming and amazing years of my life." Moreover, she recalled that at the AMH campus, "Mrs. Edna Ashmeade and Mrs. Gretel Ashley reminded the student nurses when doing an assignment to 'leave their mark—our Seventh-day Adventist Christian brand.'" This graduate continued to say, "I still try to maintain that level of working and caring for my patients."

Another graduate stated, "It's hard to believe it's been forty-five years since I left WIC; it's still so vivid a memory and relations so strong. I would choose to repeat it all over again if given a choice."

One more graduate commented, "Indeed we were blessed and didn't know it then..." She also remarked that it was "God's handiwork in establishing Northern Caribbean University Department of Nursing."

Summary

The graduates have made and continue to make an outstanding impact on the lives of individuals. They made and continue to make extraordinary contributions to the world. They have represented and continue to represent Northern Caribbean University with distinction. Most importantly, they have been and are living witnesses for God who has guided their footsteps. And so, there are many roads yet to be travelled serving God and humanity, going wherever He leads, and giving Him all the praise, honour, and glory!

CHAPTER 20

Epilogue — Almost Fifty Years Later

Facilities

Today, Northern Caribbean University (NCU) Department of Nursing is headquartered in Mandeville, Jamaica, the main campus for the university. The department is housed in the Hyacinth Chen Building that was constructed from a donation of over 247 million dollars by Michael Lee-Chin, chairman of the National Commercial Bank of Jamaica, in honour of his mother. This state-of-the-art building, which was opened in August 2008, houses five classrooms, one Anatomy and Physiology Laboratory, five nursing skills laboratories, and one lecture theatre as well as student and faculty lounges. The NCU Department of Nursing also operates a secondary hub at the Kingston campus. Although in 1971 the Kingston campus was originally located on the Andrews Memorial Hospital property at 27 Hope Road, in 2004 the NCU Kingston campus was relocated to 63 Half Way Tree Road. This facility is shared with the NCU Department of Continuing and Professional Education. There are several classrooms, computer rooms, a library, and nursing skills laboratories at this site.[1]

Nursing Programmes

NCU continues to offer the generic baccalaureate nursing programme but also offers the RN-BSc upgrade programme for those who are registered nurses and want to obtain their BSc degree. The dramatic growth in applications and enrolment over the years has been astonishing. Today, NCU receives over 300 applications per year from those who want a BSc degree in nursing. Ninety-five per cent of the applicants apply for the generic programme, and five per cent apply for the RN-BSc upgrade programme. Unfortunately, the NCU Department of Nursing can admit only about 120 applicants per year based on availability of clinical sites and the number of faculty and clinical preceptors. For the 2018–2019 academic year, a total of 435 students were enrolled in the two nursing programmes. Ninety per cent of the students are from Jamaica; others are from the Caribbean region. There is an active NCU Student Nurses Association.[2]

Curriculum

The generic baccalaureate nursing programme is four years of full-time study, including summers. The RN-BSc upgrade programme is tailored to meet the needs of the registered nurse who requires additional theoretical and clinical experiences to obtain the BSc degree in nursing. Some of the courses in the RN-BSc upgrade programme are taught online.[3] Today, there is greater emphasis on using physical examination skills as a part of health assessment, care of older persons, and applying research to practice than in the 1970s. There is also more emphasis on gaining knowledge about applied statistics, information technology, and legal responsibilities.[4]

The curriculum is arranged for the students to spend their freshman and sophomore years in Mandeville. During the freshman year, students spend much of their time studying the biological, natural, and social sciences. However, they also do what is called Wellness Rotation. The students are assigned to facilities such as schools and day care centres where they observe and are engaged with well, non-hospitalized individuals. Through this avenue and classroom instruction they learn what is considered to be a state of good health and how to optimize it before learning about illnesses and diseases. Hospital clinical experiences begin in the sophomore year accompanied by theoretical instruction. The junior year is split between Mandeville and Kingston for classroom instruction and clinical rotations, whereas the senior year is based in Kingston for all learning experiences.

Administrators at University Hospital of the West Indies continue to provide access to our student nurses for clinical practice. We also have access to private health care facilities. In addition, NCU Department of Nursing has a Memorandum of Understanding with each of the four Regional Health Authorities to access government-operated hospitals and clinics across much of the island to obtain the necessary diversity of clinical experiences.[5]

Faculty

In the early years of the baccalaureate programme, the Department of Nursing relied heavily on foreign missionaries. Today, the cadre of full-time faculty are from Jamaica and have the appropriate credentials to teach in a university-based, baccalaureate nursing programme. Faculty are qualified in various areas of nursing practice via graduate degrees, specialty certifications, and clinical practice. All nursing faculty have at least a master's degree. The director, Heather Fletcher, has a PhD in nursing. The Department of Nursing also engages the services of clinical preceptors who complement the NCU nursing faculty to maintain a faculty-student ratio of 1:15 in keeping with the standard of the Nursing Council of Jamaica. The recruitment of faculty is an ongoing challenge.[6]

Licensure and Accreditation

Student nurses who have completed the generic baccalaureate nursing programme sit the Regional Examination for Nurse Registration which qualifies them to practice in any of the English-speaking Caribbean Islands. They are also eligible to sit licensure examinations in the United States, United Kingdom, Canada, and other parts of the world.[7] The nursing programmes are accredited by the Nursing Council of Jamaica, the Seventh-day Adventist Accrediting Association, and the University Council of Jamaica.[8]

American Heart Association Training Programmes

NCU became an authorized American Heart Association (AHA) Training Center in 2012. The functions of the AHA Training Programmes are to prepare and certify health professionals and lay persons in the practice of Basic Life Support, Advanced Cardiac Life Support, Heartsaver® CPR and First Aid courses.[9] Since implementation of this programme, it has accounted for the training of more than 2,500 participants, including registered nurses, medical doctors, student nurses, and first responders such as fire marshals and security officers. The various courses are open to the community.[10]

Graduates

The Department of Nursing prepares graduates who meet world-class standards as competent practitioners whose service demonstrates a Christian philosophy of providing wholistic care to diverse peoples, nations, and cultures.[11] From 1974 to 2018, NCU conferred the degree, Bachelor of Science in Nursing, on more than 1,800 graduates.[12]

The nurse's pin that a graduate wears on his/her uniform after earning a BSc degree in nursing from Northern Caribbean University.
Photo: Courtesy of the University.

NOTES

CHAPTER ONE

1. Alton B. Marshalleck (former business manager, Andrews Memorial Hospital) in discussion with Karen J. Radke, June 29, 2014.

2. Howard and Doreen English (grand-nephew and virtual son, and daughter-in-law of H. S. Walters), *Celebrating a Life of Dedicated Service: Hiram Sebastian Walters, O.D., D.D., July 15, 1917–October 2, 2001*, (Apopka, Florida: The Rugless Group Inc., 2001), 2; Copy of funeral programme provided by Alton B. and Edith G. Marshalleck to Karen J. Radke, December 23, 2015.

3. Ibid., 2, 4.

4. Staff of the Northern Caribbean University (NCU) Library, "Humility of a Giant," 1. Unpublished document, 1991, provided by Shannette Smith (administrative assistant, NCU Library) to Heather F. Fletcher, December 9, 2015.

5. English, *Celebrating a Life of Dedicated Service*, 4.

6. Arthur E. Sutton, *Jamaica: Island of Miracles* (Nashville, Tennessee: Southern Publishing Association, 1966), 23.

7. Ibid., 7.

8. Ibid., 23.

9. Ibid., 23–24.

10. Ibid., 24.

11. Alton B. Marshalleck (former business manager, Andrews Memorial Hospital) in discussion with Karen J. Radke, June 29, 2014.

12. M. G. Nembhard, "Historic Union Session: West Indies Achieves Conference Status," *The Inter-American Messenger*, 45, no. 9 (1968): 3, https://1ref.us/tl (accessed January 6, 2020).

13. *Seventh-day Adventist Yearbook 1969* (Washington, D. C.: Review and Herald Publishing Association, 1969), 365, data reported for 1968, https://1ref.us/tm (accessed January 6, 2020).

14. Ibid., 374.

15. Rose Henry Morgan (Class of 1975 and daughter of Matron Mildred Henry) in e-mail message to Karen J. Radke, July 17, 2016.

16. Hermi Hyacinth Hewitt, *Trailblazers in Nursing Education: A Caribbean Perspective, 1946–1986* (Kingston, Jamaica: Canoe Press, University of the West Indies, Mona, 2002), 104–165.

17. Gertrude Hildegarde Swaby (prominent leader in nursing education) in discussions with Karen J. Radke, 1972–1973.

18. Alton B. Marshalleck (former business manager, Andrews Memorial Hospital) in discussion with Karen J. Radke, June 29, 2014.

19. Wanda Sample, ed., "West Indies Union," *Inter-American News Flashes,"* no. 154 (1976): 1, https://1ref.us/tn (accessed January 6, 2020).

20. M. G. Nembhard, "Special Recognition," *Inter-American News Flashes,"* no. 2 (1970): 1, https://1ref.us/z9 (accessed February 4, 2020).

21. E. H. Thomas, "GC President Visits West Indies Union: Jamaica," *General Conference of Seventh-day Adventists Inter-American Division News Flashes,"* no. 406 (1990): 3, https://1ref.us/to (accessed January 6, 2020).

22. "Hiram S. Walters Resource Centre: History," https://1ref.us/za (accessed February 4, 2020).

23. English, *Celebrating a Life of Dedicated Service*, 5

24. Staff of the Northern Caribbean University (NCU) Library, "Humility of a Giant," 1, revised August 4, 2001.

25. English, *Celebrating a Life of Dedicated Service*, 1.

CHAPTER TWO

1. Allen Moon, "Shall We Have a School in Jamaica?" *Advent Review and Sabbath Herald* 75, no. 2 (1898): 32, https://1ref.us/tp (accessed January 6, 2020).

2. *Seventh-day Adventist Yearbook for 1893* (Battle Creek, MI: General Conference Association of Seventh-day Adventists, 1893), 64, https://1ref.us/tq (accessed January 6, 2020).

3. W. A. Spicer, "The Jamaica Conference," *Advent Review and Sabbath Herald* 80, no. 11 (1903): 16, https://1ref.us/tr (accessed January 6, 2020).

4. *Seventh-day Adventist Yearbook for 1904* (Washington, DC: The General Conference of Seventh-day Adventists, 1904), 74, data reported for 1903, https://1ref.us/ts (accessed January 6, 2020).

5. Hubert Fletcher, "Synopsis of the Message in Jamaica," *Advent Review and Sabbath Herald* 82, no. 9 (1905): 12, https://1ref.us/tt (accessed January 6, 2020).

6. Trevor O'Reggio, "Exploring the Factors That Shaped the Early Adventist Mission to Jamaica," *Journal of the Adventist Theological Society*, 19/ 1–2 (2008): 235, https://1ref.us/tu (accessed January 6, 2020).

7. Spicer, "The Jamaica Conference," 16.

8. *Seventh-day Adventist Yearbook for 1904*, 74.

9.   Ibid., 11.

10.   Spicer, "The Jamaica Conference," 16.

11.   Ibid.

12.   Geo. F. Enoch, "An Industrial School for the West Indies," *Caribbean Watchman* 4, no. 9 (1906): 2, https://1ref.us/tv (accessed January 6, 2020).

13.   Geo. F. Enoch, "An Industrial School for the West Indies," *Advent Review and Sabbath Herald* 83, no. 32 (1906): 13, https://1ref.us/tw (accessed January 6, 2020).

14.   Enoch, "An Industrial School for the West Indies," *Caribbean Watchman*, 2, 12.

15.   "Jamaica Conference Directory," *Jamaica Record* 2, no. 7 (1906): 4, https://1ref.us/tx (accessed January 6, 2020).

16.   J. B. Beckner, "Jamaica," *Advent Review and Sabbath Herald* 83, no. 29 (1906): 15, https://1ref.us/ty (accessed January 6, 2020).

17.   Enoch, "An Industrial School for the West Indies," *Caribbean Watchman*, 2.

18.   "Testimonial of Maude-Peart-Goulbourne as told to Garnet Weir in January, 1972," quoted in Trevor O'Reggio, "Exploring the Factors That Shaped the Early Adventist Mission to Jamaica," *Journal of the Adventist Theological Society*, 19/ 1–2 (2008): 249, https://1ref.us/tz (accessed January 6, 2020).

19.   Hubert Fletcher, "The Jamaica Conference," *Advent Review and Sabbath Herald* 83, no. 6 (1906): 19, https://1ref.us/u0 (access January 6, 2020).

20.   Beckner, "Jamaica," 15.

21.   N. Johnston, "A Visit to Willowdeen," *Jamaica Record* 2, no. 7 (1906): 3, https://1ref.us/tx (accessed January 6, 2020).

22.   I. H. Evans, "The East Caribbean Conference," *Advent Review and Sabbath Herald* 83, no. 31 (1906); 18, https://1ref.us/u1 (accessed January 6, 2020).

23.   *1907 Yearbook of the Seventh-day Adventist Denomination* (Washington, DC: Review and Herald Publishing Association, 1907), 97, data reported for 1906, https://1ref.us/u2 (accessed January 6, 2020).

24.   S. A. Wellman, ed., "The 4th Annual Session of the East Caribbean Conference," *Caribbean Watchman* 4, no. 8 (1906): 12, https://1ref.us/u3 (accessed January 6, 2020).

25.   Geo. F. Enoch, "The West Indian Training School," *Jamaica Record* 2, no. 10 (1906): 1, https://1ref.us/u4 (accessed January 6, 2020).

26.   Ibid., 2.

27.   Geo. F. Enoch, "The West Indian Training School," *Advent Review and Sabbath Herald* 83, no. 45 (1906): 14, https://1ref.us/u5 (accessed January 6, 2020).

28.   General Conference of Seventh-day Adventists Executive Committee, July 24, 1906, [Minutes], s.vv. "Jamaica, School:" 159, https://1ref.us/u6 (accessed January 6, 2020).

29.   General Conference of Seventh-day Adventists Executive Committee, October 10, 1906, [Minutes], s.vv. "C. O. L. for West Indies:" 211, https://1ref.us/u6

(accessed January 6, 2020). 30. Elder Enoch has informed us [Jamaica Conference personnel] ..., *Jamaica Record* 2, no. 10 (1906): 2, https://1ref.us/u4 (accessed January 6, 2020).

31. C. B. Hughes, "The West Indian Training School," *General Conference Bulletin* 6, no. 20 (1909): 339, https://1ref.us/u7 (accessed January 6, 2020).

32. *1908 Yearbook of the Seventh-day Adventist Denomination* (Washington, D. C.: Review and Herald Publishing Association, 1908), 149, data reported for 1907, https://1ref.us/u8 (accessed January 6, 2020).

33. General Conference of Seventh-day Adventists Executive Committee, November 20, 1906, [Minutes], s.vv. "Jamaica, Professor Hughes:" 226, https://1ref.us/u6 (accessed January 6, 2020).

34. C. B. Hughes, "The West Indian Training School," 339.

35. Floyd Greenleaf, *The Seventh-day Adventist Church in Latin America and the Caribbean, Volume I, Let the Earth Hear His Voice* (Berrien Springs, MI: Andrews University Press, 1992), 143.

36. C. B. Hughes, "The West Indian Training School," 339.

37. Johnston, "A Visit to Willowdeen," 3.

38. Mrs. C. B. Hughes, "The School Work in Jamaica," *Advent Review and Sabbath Herald* 85, no. 14 (1908): 29, https://1ref.us/u9 (accessed January 6, 2020).

39. *1908 Yearbook*, 149, data reported for 1907.

40. C. B. Hughes, "The West Indian Training School," 339.

41. *1908 Yearbook*, 149, data reported for 1907.

42. General Conference of Seventh-day Adventists Executive Committee, February 7, 1907, [Minutes], s.vv. "Jamaica School:" 242, https://1ref.us/ua (accessed January 6, 2020).

43. Ibid.

44. *1908 Yearbook*, 149, data reported for 1907.

45. Greenleaf, *The Seventh-day Adventist Church*, 143.

46. General Conference of Seventh-day Adventists Executive Committee, September 19, 1907, [Minutes], s.vv. "West Indian School:" 343, https://1ref.us/ua (accessed January 6, 2020).

47. General Conference of Seventh-day Adventists Executive Committee, September 25, 1907, [Minutes], s.vv. "West Indian School:" 350, https://1ref.us/ua (accessed January 6, 2020).

48. C. B. Hughes, "The West Indian Training School," 339–340.

49. Ibid., 340.

50. *1910 Yearbook of the Seventh-day Adventist Denomination* (Washington, DC, Review and Herald Publishing Association, 1910), 160, data reported for 1909, https://1ref.us/ub (accessed January 6, 2020).

51. "College History," *BULLETIN West Indies College 1973–75* (Mandeville, Jamaica: West Indies College Press, 1973), 7.

52. Beverly Henry (former assistant vice-president of student services and records, and director of protocol, West Indies College) in e-mail message to Karen J. Radke, April 16, 2017.

53. Don F. Neufeld, ed., *Seventh-day Adventist Encyclopedia*, Second Revised Edition, Volume M-Z, Commentary Reference Series, Volume 10, s.vv. "West Indies College" (Maryland: Review and Herald Publishing Association, 1996), 866.

54. *1918 Yearbook of the Seventh-day Adventist Denomination* (Washington, DC: Review and Herald Publishing Association, 1918), 179, https://1ref.us/uc (accessed January 6, 2020).

55. "WITC," *The College Echo*, July 12, 1938, 1, 4 (Mandeville, Jamaica: West Indian Training College Press, 1938), quoted in Anthon C. Francis, "Development of West Indies College, 1907–1980: A Historical Study" (PhD dissertation, Andrews University, 1984), 74, https://1ref.us/ud (accessed January 6, 2020).

56. Neufeld, *Seventh-day Adventist Encyclopedia*, s.vv. "West Indies College," 867.

57. Hubert Fletcher, "Report of the Jamaica Conference: Educational," *General Conference Bulletin* 9, no. 15 (1922): 348, https://1ref.us/ue (accessed January 6, 2020).

58. "WITC," *The College Echo*, July 12, 1938, 1, 4 (Mandeville, Jamaica: West Indian Training College Press, 1938), quoted in Anthon C. Francis, "Development of West Indies College, 1907–1980: A Historical Study" (PhD dissertation, Andrews University, 1984), 74, https://1ref.us/ud (accessed January 6, 2020).

59. General Conference of Seventh-day Adventists Executive Committee, April 15, 1918, [Minutes], s.vv. "West Indian Union School:" 11, https://1ref.us/uf (accessed January 6, 2020).

60. General Conference of Seventh-day Adventists Executive Committee, February 19, 1918, [Minutes], s.vv. "C B Hughes—W I U School:" 732, https://1ref.us/uf (accessed January 6, 2020).

61. "General Conference Proceedings: Distribution of Labor," *General Conference Bulletin* 8, no. 12 (1918): 178, https://1ref.us/ug (accessed January 6, 2020).

62. West Indies College, *Palm Leaves 69* (Mandeville, Jamaica: United Student Movement, West Indies College Press, 1969), 16. Northern Caribbean University Hiram S. Walters Resource Centre, Mandeville, Jamaica.

63. Ibid.

64. General Conference of Seventh-day Adventists Executive Committee, February 19, 1918, 732.

65. *Yearbook of the Seventh-day Adventist Denomination for 1919* (Washington, DC: Review and Herald Publishing Association, 1919): 212, data reported for 1918, https://1ref.us/uh (accessed January 6, 2020).

66. West Indies College, *Palm Leaves 69* (Mandeville, Jamaica: United Student Movement, West Indies College Press, 1969), 18. Northern Caribbean University Hiram S. Walters Resource Centre, Mandeville, Jamaica.

67. West Indies College, *Palm Leaves 69*, 17.

68. Neufeld, *Seventh-day Adventist Encyclopedia*, s.vv. "West Indies College," 867.

69. General Conference of Seventh-day Adventists Executive Committee, January 31, 1919, [Minutes], s.vv. "W H Wineland to Jamaica:" 224, https://1ref.us/ui (accessed January 6, 2020).

70. *1920 Yearbook of the Seventh-day Adventist Denomination* (Washington, DC: Review and Herald Publishing Association, 1920), 240, data reported for 1919, https://1ref.us/uj (accessed January 6, 2020).

71. West Indies College, *Palm Leaves 69*, 17.

72. Ibid., 18.

73. C. J. Boyd, "The West Indian Training School," *Inter-American Messenger* 1, no. 2 (1924): 3, https://1ref.us/uk (accessed January 6, 2020).

74. Neufeld, *Seventh-day Adventist Encyclopedia*, s.vv. "West Indies College," 867.

75. Cleve Henriques, "Our School," *Jamaica Visitor* 8, no. 1 (1934): 6, https://1ref.us/ul (accessed January 6, 2020).

76. West Indies College, *Palm Leaves 69*, 18.

77. Ivy J. Andrade, "The O.S. & T.A. Meeting," *Jamaica Visitor* 1, no. 6 (1927): 4, 5, https://1ref.us/um (accessed January 6, 2020).

78. Laura F. Rathbun, ed., "Mandeville," *Jamaica Visitor* 1, no. 12 (1927): 4, https://1ref.us/un (accessed January 6, 2020).

79. Susan Long Gordon (director of alumni relations and planned giving, Northern Caribbean University) in discussion with Dr. Aston Barnes, alumnus of West Indies College. Susan Long Gordon in e-mail message to Karen J. Radke, January 10, 2017.

80. F. O. Rathbun, "Commencement Exercises at W.I.T.C.," *Jamaica Visitor* 1, no. 11 (1927): 5, https://1ref.us/uo (accessed January 6, 2020).

81. Rayon Daley, "Annals of NCU 2," https://1ref.us/up (accessed January 6, 2020).

82. R. J. Sype, "The First Semester, 1928," *Jamaica Visitor* 3, no. 3 (1928): 8, https://1ref.us/uq (accessed January 6, 2020).

83. R. J. Sype, "From the College," *Jamaica Visitor* 3, no. 2 (1928): 4, https://1ref.us/ur (accessed January 6, 2020).

84. R. E. Shafer, "West Indian Training College," *Jamaica Visitor* 8, no. 3 (1934): 6–8, https://1ref.us/us (accessed January 6, 2020).

85. C. E. Andross, ed., "West Indian Training College," *Jamaica Visitor* 11, no. 4 (1936): 6, https://1ref.us/ut (accessed January 6, 2020).

86. Henriques, "Our School," 7.

87. Hughes, "The West Indian Training School," 340.

88. Mrs. E. E. Andross, ed., Professor W. H. Wineland in a personal letter, *Inter-American Messenger* 2, no. 2 (1925): 4, https://1ref.us/uu(accessed January 6, 2020).

89. Boyd, "The West Indian Training School," 3.

90. W. H. Wineland, "Another Miracle of Missions," *Inter-American Messenger* 2, no. 5 (1925): 3, https://1ref.us/uv (accessed January 6, 2020).

91. Neufeld, *Seventh-day Adventist Encyclopedia*, s.vv. "West Indies College," 867.

92. College Rhetoric Class, "W. I. T. C. Items," *Jamaica Visitor* 1, no. 4 (1926): 6, https://1ref.us/uw (accessed January 6, 2020).

93. *Seventh-day Adventist Yearbook for 1971* (Washington DC: Review and Herald Publishing Association, 1971), 387, https://1ref.us/ux (accessed January 6, 2020).

94. A. N. Shafer, "Some Classes Taught at W. I. T. C.: Bible," *Jamaica Visitor* 13, no. 10 (1938): 2, https://1ref.us/uy (accessed January 6, 2020).

95. Henriques, "Our School," 6.

96. O. W. Tucker, "West Indian Training College," *Jamaica Visitor* 3, no. 15 (1929): 5, https://1ref.us/uz (accessed January 6, 2020).

97. Ibid., 8.

98. Business Manager, "West Indian Training College," *Jamaica Visitor* 5, no. 2 (1930): 7, https://1ref.us/v0 (accessed January 6, 2020).

99. R. E. Shafer, "West Indian Training College," *Jamaica Visitor* 6, no. 1 (1931): 7, https://1ref.us/v1 (accessed January 6, 2020).

100. W. H. Wineland, "West Indian Training College," *Jamaica Visitor* 1, no. 6 (1927): 4, https://1ref.us/um (accessed January 6, 2020).

101. F. O. Rathbun, ed., "W. I. T. C. News Notes," *Jamaica Visitor* 1, no. 8 (1927): 5, https://1ref.us/v2 (accessed January 6, 2020).

102. B. G. Butherus, "West Indian Training College," *British West Indies Union Visitor* 3, no. 10 (1946): 2, https://1ref.us/v3 (accessed January 6, 2020).

103. B. G. Butherus, "West Indian Training College: Happenings of the College," *British West Indies Union Visitor* 4, no. 7 (1947): 7, https://1ref.us/v4 (accessed January 6, 2020).

104. A. N. Shafer, "Ministerial Improvement Association," *Jamaica Visitor* 13, no. 10 (1938): 4, https://1ref.us/uy (accessed January 6, 2020).

105. F. S. Thompson, "West Indian Training College," *Jamaica Visitor* 15, no. 1 (1940): 8, https://1ref.us/v5 (accessed January 6, 2020).

106. Tucker, "West Indian Training College," 5. Additional information provided by Leonarda Dowdie-McKenzie in e-mail message to Karen J. Radke, October 4, 2019.

107. B. L. Archbold, "West Indian Training College," *Jamaica Visitor* 11, no. 3 (1936): 6, https://1ref.us/v6 (accessed January 6, 2020).

108. F. S. Thompson, untitled, *The College Echo*, May 25, 1936, 1, 4, quoted in Anthon C. Francis, *Development of West Indies College 1907–1960: A Historical Study* (PhD dissertation, Andrews University, 1984), 254, https://1ref.us/ud (accessed January 6, 2020).

109. C. E. Andross, ed., "W. I. T. C. News," *Jamaica Visitor* 11, no. 7 (1936): 6, https://1ref.us/v7 (accessed January 6, 2020).

110. Susan Long Gordon (director of alumni relations and planned giving, Northern Caribbean University) in e-mail message to Heather F. Fletcher, November 7, 2016.

111. Dorothy M. Comm, "The West Indies College Yearbook—Palm Leaves," *West Indies Union Visitor* 17, no. 4 (1960): 6, https://1ref.us/v8 (accessed January , 2020).

112. O. W. Tucker, "West Indian Training College," *Jamaica Visitor* 5, no. 1 (1930): 7, https://1ref.us/v9 (accessed January 6, 2020).

113. H. D. Isaac, "W. I. T. College: Damage by Fire," *Jamaica Visitor* 10, no. 11 (1935): 3–4, https://1ref.us/va (accessed January 6, 2020).

114. Robert H. Pierson, ed., "Here and There in the Union: W. I. T. C. Remodeling Programme," *British West Indies Union Visitor* 3, no. 8 (1946): 6, https://1ref.us/vb (accessed January 6, 2020).

115. B. G. Butherus, "Building a Normal School at the West Indian Training College," *British West Indies Union Visitor* 3, no. 4 (1946): 1, https://1ref.us/vc (accessed January 6, 2020).

116. Glenn Calkins, "Building for God," *British West Indies Union Visitor* 8, no. 4 (1951): 1, https://1ref.us/vd (accessed January 6, 2020).

117. Glenn Calkins, "Must We Stop Evangelizing?" *Inter-American Division Messenger* 28, no. 10 (1951): 1, https://1ref.us/ve (accessed January 6, 2020).

118. H. E. Nembhard, "By Sacrifice," *British West Indies Union Visitor* 8, no. 4 (1951): 4, https://1ref.us/vd (accessed February 4, 2020).

119. B. G. Butherus, "Our Day of Opportunity," *British West Indies Union Visitor* 8, no. 4 (1951): 4, https://1ref.us/vd (accessed January 6, 2020).

120. Ibid.

121. Joe Fletcher, "Arise! Gather—Give, and Build!" *British West Indies Union Visitor* 8, no. 4 (1951): 5, 6, https://1ref.us/vd (accessed January 6, 2020).

122. R. W. Numbers, "Sincere Sympathy," *British West Indies Union Visitor* 8, no. 9 (1951): 1, https://1ref.us/vf (accessed January 6, 2020).

123. R. W. Numbers, "On the 'Hill'," *British West Indies Union Visitor* 8, no. 9 (1951): 2, https://1ref.us/vf (accessed January 6, 2020).

124. M. J. Sorenson, "Progress on Building Programme at W I T C," *British West Indies Union Visitor* 10, no. 7 (1953): 3, https://1ref.us/vg (accessed January 6, 2020).

125. M. J. Sorenson, "A Glimpse at W. I. T. C.," *British West Indies Union Visitor* 11, no. 10 (1954): 3, https://1ref.us/vh (accessed January 6, 2020).

126. A. C. Stockhausen, "Part II: The President's Report at the Second Session of the British West Indies Union, June 1–4, 1956: Building," *British West Indies Union Visitor* 13, nos. 7, 8, & 9 (1956): 2, https://1ref.us/vi (accessed January 6, 2020).

127. R. S. Blackburn, "New Girl's Dormitory at W. I. T. C.," *British West Indies Union Visitor* 14, nos. 5 & 6 (1957): 1, https://1ref.us/vj (accessed January 6, 2020).

128. M. G. Nembhard, ed., "College Highlights," *British West Indies Union Visitor* 21, no. 3 (1964): 8, https://1ref.us/vk (accessed January 6, 2020).

129. Butherus, "West Indian Training College," 2.

130. R. Rubin Widmer, "West Indies College Ministerial Training Programme," *West Indies Union Visitor* 17, no. 3 (1960): 6, https://1ref.us/vl (accessed January 6, 2020).

131. "College History," BULLETIN *West Indies College 1973–75*, 7.

132. Neufeld, *Seventh-day Adventist Encyclopedia*, s.vv. "West Indies College," 867.

133. General Conference of Seventh-day Adventists Executive Committee, July 7, 1960, [Minutes], s.vv. "West Indies College—Status:," 635.

134. Leif Kr. Tobiassen, "General Conference Endorses," *West Indies Union Visitor* 17, no. 3 (1960): 6, https://1ref.us/vl (accessed January 6, 2020).

135. Walton J. Brown, "An Educational Mizpah," *Inter-American Messenger* 44, no. 8 (1967): 2, https://1ref.us/vm (accessed January 6, 2020).

136. M. G. Nembhard, "West Indies Union Celebrates Three Anniversaries," *Inter-American Messenger* 47, no. 5 (1970): 10, https://1ref.us/vn (accessed January 6, 2020).

137. "College History," BULLETIN *West Indies College 1973–75*, 7.

138. "Former NCU (WIC) President Dies," *Northern Caribbean University News*, https://1ref.us/vo (accessed January 6, 2020).

139. "West Indies College: Courses Offered," *Palm Leaves 74* (Mandeville, Jamaica: United Student Movement, 1974), 75. Northern Caribbean University Hiram S. Walters Resource Centre, Mandeville, Jamaica.

140. Nembhard, "West Indies Union Celebrates Three Anniversaries," 10.

141. Karen J. Radke, *Notes on Jamaica: 1972–1973*. Unpublished document.

CHAPTER THREE

1. R. W. Numbers, ed., "History of Andrews Memorial Hospital and Clinic," *British West Indies Union Visitor* 7, no. 2 (1950): 3, https://1ref.us/vp (accessed January 6, 2020).

2. *1945 Yearbook of the Seventh-day Adventist Denomination* (Washington D.C.: Review and Herald Publishing Association, 1945), 119, data reported for 1944, https://1ref.us/vq (accessed January 6, 2020).

3. Clifford R. Anderson, "Medical Work in Jamaica," *Inter-American Division Messenger* 23, no. 8 (1946): 4, https://1ref.us/vr (accessed January 6, 2020).

4. Ibid.

5. Effie A. James, asst. ed., "The Medical Work," *Inter-American Division Messenger* 22, no. 7 (1945): 4, https://1ref.us/vs (accessed January 6, 2020).

6. Bobbie Jane Van Dolson and Leo R. Van Dolson, eds., *Seventh-day Adventist Encyclopedia*, Second Revised Edition, Volume A–L, Commentary Reference Series, Volume 10, (Maryland: Review and Herald Publishing Association, 1996), s.vv. "John Nevins Andrews," 68.

7. James, "The Medical Work," 4.

8. Robert H. Pierson, ed., "The New Sanitarium," *British West Indies Union Visitor* 1, no. 5 (1944): 3, https://1ref.us/vt (accessed January 6, 2020).

9. Kenneth H. Wood, ed., "Deaths," *Adventist Review*, 159, no. 5 (1982): 15, https://1ref.us/vu (accessed January 6, 2020).

10. Pierson, "The New Sanitarium," 3.

11. Wood, "Deaths," *Adventist Review* 159, no.5 (1982): 15.

12. Anderson, "Medical Work in Jamaica," 4.

13. Ibid.

14. "Acting Gov. Opens Andrews Memorial Clinic," *Gleaner* (Kingston, Jamaica), December 13, 1945, quoted in *British West Indies Union Visitor* 3, no. 1 (1946): 5, https://1ref.us/vv (accessed January 6, 2020).

15. Anderson, "Medical Work in Jamaica," 4.

16. R. H. Pierson, "Arrivals and Departures," *Inter-American Division Messenger* 23, no. 2 (1946): 4, https://1ref.us/vw (accessed January 6, 2020).

17. Clifford R. Anderson, "Business Manager Arrives," *British West Indies Union Visitor* 2, no. 4 (1945): 3, https://1ref.us/vx (accessed January 6, 2020).

18. James, "The Medical Work," 4.

19. "Acting Gov. Opens Andrews Memorial Clinic," 5.

20. Clifford R. Anderson, "The Clinic Is Going Up Too!" *British West Indies Union Visitor* 2, no. 4 (1945): 3, https://1ref.us/vx (accessed January 6, 2020).

21. Ouida E. Spleen Westney (Class of 1950, Andrews Memorial Hospital and Clinic School of Nursing) in e-mail message to Karen J. Radke, May 18, 2017.

22. Anderson, "The Clinic Is Going Up Too!" 3.

23. Clifford R. Anderson, "Hospital Building Programme," *British West Indies Union Visitor* 2, no. 4 (1945): 3, https://1ref.us/vx (accessed January 6, 2020).

24. Anderson, "Medical Work in Jamaica," 4.

25. *1945 Yearbook of the Seventh-day Adventist Denomination* (Washington, D.C.: Review and Herald Publishing Association, 1945), 120, data reported for 1944, https://1ref.us/vq (accessed January 6, 2020).

26. Anderson, "Business Manager Arrives," 3.

27. Ibid.

28. Van Dolson and Van Dolson, *Seventh-day Adventist Encyclopedia*, s.vv. "Andrews Memorial Hospital," 69.

29. Church History Committee 2006 (Walton Reid, Rose Omphroy, Audrey Tomlinson, and Yvonne Gunning), "Partial History of the Andrews Memorial Seventh-day Adventist Church," 1, https://1ref.us/vy (accessed January 6, 2020).

30. Anderson, "Medical Work in Jamaica," 4.

31. Ouida E. Spleen Westney (Class of 1950, Andrews Memorial Hospital and Clinic School of Nursing) in discussion with Karen J. Radke, May 17, 2017.

32. Anderson, "Business Manager Arrives," 3.

33. Clifford R. Anderson, "Our Nursing School Opens," *British West Indies Union Visitor* 2, no. 4 (1945): 3, https://1ref.us/vx (accessed January 6, 2020).

34. Rose Henry Morgan (daughter of Mildred Richards Henry who graduated in 1948 from Andrews Memorial Hospital and Clinic School of Nursing) in e-mail message to Karen J. Radke, February 13, 2015.

35. Anderson, "Our Nursing School Opens," 3.

36. Anderson, "Business Manager Arrives," 3.

37. D. Lois Burnett (associate secretary for nursing education and nursing service, Medical Department, General Conference of Seventh-day Adventists), "Andrews Memorial Hospital and Clinic," (unpublished document, Box 2, Folder 2, Muriel E. Chapman Collection: The History of Seventh-day Adventist Nursing [collection 270], Center for Adventist Research, James White Library, Andrews University, Berrien Springs, Michigan), 1. Consultation visit regarding AMH School of Nursing, January 15–24, 1946. Document sent by Tamara Karr, administrative assistant, Center for Adventist Research, in e-mail message to Karen J. Radke, November 13, 2015. Document used with permission of Jim Ford, associate director, May 24, 2017.

38. Anderson, "Our Nursing School Opens," 3.

39. Anderson, "Medical Work in Jamaica," 4.

40. Clifford R. Anderson and F. Ruth Mitchell, "Andrews Memorial School of Nursing," (unpublished document, Box 2, Folder 2, Muriel E. Chapman Collection: The History of Seventh-day Adventist Nursing [collection 270], Center for Adventist Research, James White Library, Andrews University, Berrien Springs, Michigan), 2. Letter to Miss D. Lois Burnett, associate secretary, Nursing Education and Nursing Service, Medical Department, General Conference of Seventh-day Adventists. Document sent by Tamara Karr, administrative assistant, Center for Adventist Research, in e-mail message to Karen J. Radke, November 13, 2015. Document used with permission of Jim Ford, associate director, May 24, 2017.

41. Anderson, "Our Nursing School Opens," 3.

42. Ouida E. Spleen Westney (Class of 1950, Andrews Memorial Hospital and Clinic School of Nursing) in e-mail message to Karen J. Radke, July 18, 2016.

43. Anderson and Mitchell, "Andrews Memorial School of Nursing," 1.

44. Robert H. Pierson, ed., "Andrews Memorial Hospital School of Nursing Recognized by Government," *British West Indies Union Visitor* 3, no. 3 (1946): 2, https://1ref.us/vz (accessed January 6, 2020).

45. Ouida E. Spleen Westney (Class of 1950, Andrews Memorial Hospital and Clinic School of Nursing) in e-mail message to Heather F. Fletcher, June 26, 2016.

46. Robert H. Pierson, "Medical Workers Leave Union," *British West Indies Union Visitor* 3, no. 7 (1946): 4, https://1ref.us/w0 (accessed January 6, 2020).

47. Robert H. Pierson, "Comings and Goings in the Union," *British West Indies Union Visitor* 3, no. 4 (1946): 3, https://1ref.us/vc (accessed January 6, 2020).

48. Pierson, "Medical Workers Leave Union," 4.

49. Anderson and Mitchell, "Andrews Memorial School of Nursing," 3.

50. Robert H. Pierson, "Welcome to Miss Mitchell," *British West Indies Union Visitor* 3, no. 8 (1946): 6, https://1ref.us/vc (accessed January 6, 2020).

51. General Conference of Seventh-day Adventists Executive Committee, June 2, 1946, [Minutes], s.vv. "Ruth Mitchell—Jamaica:" 2435, https://1ref.us/w1 (accessed January 6, 2020).

52. C. L. Torrey, ed., "The Medical Work," *Inter-American Division Messenger* 23, no. 3 (1946): 5, https://1ref.us/w2 (accessed January 6, 2020).

53. C. L. Torrey, ed., "A Symposium—Did You Know?" *Inter-American Division Messenger* 23, no. 5 (1946): 4. Dr. Clifford R. Anderson's report to the Division Committee, https://1ref.us/w3 (accessed January 6, 2020).

54. Robert H. Pierson, "Andrews Memorial Hospital Building Programme," *British West Indies Union Visitor* 3, no. 8 (1946): 6, https://1ref.us/vb (accessed January 6, 2020).

55. "Ground Break Nov. 3, 1946, for New Hospital," *The Andrews Memorial Hospital Photograph Album* page 3, Accession # AMHPA: I: 09-1, Heritage Research Center, Del E. Webb Memorial Library, Loma Linda University, Loma Linda, California, https://1ref.us/w4 (accessed January 6, 2020).

56. Numbers, "History of Andrews Memorial Hospital and Clinic," 3.

57. Van Dolson and Van Dolson, *Seventh-day Adventist Encyclopedia*, s.vv. "Andrews Memorial Hospital," 69–70.

58. S. E. White, ed., "The Andrew's Memorial Hospital Informant: Did You Know?" *British West Indies Union Visitor*, 10, no. 9 (1953): 2, https://1ref.us/w5 (accessed January 6, 2020).

59. Numbers, "History of Andrews Memorial Hospital and Clinic," 3.

60. Robert H. Pierson, ed., "News from the A. M. H.," *British West Indies Union Visitor* 5, no. 3 (1948): 2, https://1ref.us/w6 (accessed January 6, 2020).

61 Numbers, "History of Andrews Memorial Hospital and Clinic," 3.

62. Pierson, "News from the A. M. H.," 2.

63. Clifford R. Anderson, "Your Hospital Needs You," *British West Indies Union Visitor* 6, no. 7 (1949): 1, https://1ref.us/w7 (accessed January 6, 2020).

64. "Governors of Jamaica (1690–1962)," last modified June 5, 2016, https://1ref.us/w8 (accessed January 6, 2020).

65. *1948 Yearbook of the Seventh-day Adventist Denomination* (Washington, D.C.: Review and Herald Publishing Association, 1948), 279, https://1ref.us/w9 (accessed January 6, 2020).

66. *1949 Yearbook of the Seventh-day Adventist Denomination* (Washington, D. C.: Review and Herald Publishing Association, 1949), 296, https://1ref.us/wa (accessed January 6, 2020).

67. Anderson, "Your Hospital Needs You," 1.

68. Numbers, "History of Andrews Memorial Hospital and Clinic," 3.

69. Clifford R. Anderson, "Pre-Nursing at Mandeville," *British West Indies Union Visitor* 5, no. 12, (1948–1949): 6, https://1ref.us/wb (accessed January 6, 2020).

70. B. G. Butherus, "Pre-Nursing Course Offered at W. I. T. C.," *British West Indies Union Visitor* 5, no. 11 (1948): 6, https://1ref.us/wc (accessed January 6, 2020).

71. Anderson, "Pre-Nursing at Mandeville," 6.

72. *1946 Yearbook of the Seventh-day Adventist Denomination* (Washington, D.C.: Review and Herald Publishing Association, 1946), 277, https://1rcf.us/wd (accessed January 6, 2020).

73. *1948 Yearbook of the Seventh-day Adventist Denomination* (Washington, D.C.: Review and Herald Publishing Association, 1948), 285.

74. Anderson, "Pre-Nursing at Mandeville," 6.

75. Arthur H. Roth, ed., "The Andrews Memorial Hospital School of Nursing Class of 1953," *Inter-American Division Messenger* 30, no. 8 (1953): 5, refer to photograph, https://1ref.us/we (accessed January 6, 2020).

76. Numbers, "History of Andrews Memorial Hospital and Clinic," 3.

77. Anderson, "Medical Work in Jamaica," 4.

78. Numbers, "History of Andrews Memorial Hospital and Clinic," 3.

79. *1950 Yearbook of the Seventh-day Adventist Denomination* (Washington D.C.: Review and Herald Publishing Association, 1950), 131, data reported for 1949, https://1ref.us/wf (accessed January 6, 2020).

80. Numbers, "History of Andrews Memorial Hospital and Clinic," 3.

81. R. W. Numbers, ed., "Meet our Workers," *British West Indies Union Visitor* 7, no. 2 (1950): 1, https://1ref.us/vp (accessed January 6, 2020).

82. Ouida E. Spleen Westney (Class of 1950, Andrews Memorial Hospital and Clinic School of Nursing) in e-mail message to Heather F. Fletcher, June 26, 2016.

83. Numbers, "History of Andrews Memorial Hospital and Clinic," 3.

84. Ibid.

85. R. W. Numbers, ed., "Port Maria Clinic," *British West Indies Union Visitor* 7, no. 2 (1950): 4, https://1ref.us/wg (accessed January 6, 2020).

86. Linette Mitchell, *Thy Light Is Come: A Short History of the Seventh-day Adventist Church in Jamaica* (Mandeville, Jamaica, W.I.: West Indies College Press, 1990), 45.

87. A. W. N. Druitt, "Hospital News," *British West Indies Union Visitor* 7, no. 9 (1950): 4, https://1ref.us/wh (accessed January 6, 2020).

88. *1951 Yearbook of the Seventh-day Adventist Denomination* (Washington, D.C.: Review and Herald Publishing Association, 1951), 288, data reported for 1950, https://1ref.us/wi (accessed January 6, 2020).

89. R. W. Numbers, "Welcome to the Horsleys," *British West Indies Union Visitor* 7, no. 11 (1950): 4, https://1ref.us/wj (accessed January 6, 2020).

90. Alton B. Marshalleck (former business manager, Andrews Memorial Hospital) in discussion with Karen J. Radke, May 7, 2017.

91. *1952 Yearbook of the Seventh-day Adventist Denomination* (Washington, D.C.: Review and Herald Publishing Association, 1952), 278, data reported for 1951, https://1ref.us/wk (accessed January 6, 2020).

92. Ibid.

93. White, "The Andrew's Memorial Hospital Informant," 1–4.

94. Numbers, "The History of Andrews Memorial Hospital and Clinic," 3, refer to photograph.

95. "History of Andrews Memorial Hospital," 2, unpublished document provided by Alton B. Marshalleck (former business manager, Andrews Memorial Hospital) to Heather F. Fletcher, July 24, 2014.

96. White, "The Andrew's Memorial Hospital Informant," 3.

97. Ibid.

98. General Conference of Seventh-day Adventists Executive Committee, August 30, 1951, [Minutes], s.vv. "M. R. Hoehn, M. D.—Jamaica:" 495, https://1ref.us/wl (accessed January 6, 2020).

99. *1953 Yearbook of the Seventh-day Adventist Denomination* (Washington, D.C.: Review and Herald Publishing Association, 1953), 286, data reported for 1952, https://1ref.us/wm (accessed January 6, 2020).

100. Ibid.

101. Alton B. Marshalleck (former business manager, Andrews Memorial Hospital) in discussion with Karen J. Radke, June 12, 2016.

102. *1953 Yearbook of the Seventh-day Adventist Denomination*, 286, data reported for 1952.

103. D. Lois Burnett, "Visit to Andrews Memorial Hospital," (unpublished document, Box 2, Folder 2, Muriel E. Chapman Collection: The History of Seventh-day Adventist Nursing [collection 270], Center for Adventist Research, James White Library, Andrews University, Berrien Springs, Michigan), 1. Consultation visit regarding AMH, February 11–16, 1954. Document sent by Tamara Karr, administrative assistant, Center for Adventist Research, in e-mail message to Karen J. Radke, November 13, 2015. Used with permission of Jim Ford, associate director, May 24, 2017.

104. Seth Bates (library assistant, Heritage Research Center, Del E. Webb Memorial Library, Loma Linda University, California) in e-mail message to Karen J. Radke, July 26, 2016.

105. M. R. Hoehn, "Andrews Memorial Hospital," *British West Indies Union Visitor* 11, no. 4 (1954): 6, https://1ref.us/wn (accessed January 6, 2020).

106. Burnett, "Visit to Andrews Memorial Hospital," 1.

107. Roth, ed., "The Andrews Memorial Hospital School of Nursing Class of 1953," 5, refer to photograph caption.

108. Mildred Henry, *Andrews Memorial Hospital School of Assistant Nursing Bulletin* (Kingston, Jamaica, 1969), 1. Unpublished document provided by Alton B. Marshalleck (former business manager, Andrews Memorial Hospital) to Heather F. Fletcher, July 24, 2014.

109. General Conference of Seventh-day Adventists Executive Committee, February 29, 1956, [Minutes], s.vv. "Marjorie Whitney—Permanent Return:," 535, https://1ref.us/wo (accessed January 6, 2020).

110. Elizabeth Hoehn, "Andrews Memorial Hospital—News Notes," *British West Indies Union Visitor* 13, no. 2 (1956): 3, https://1ref.us/wf (accessed January 6, 2020).

111. Ibid.

112. Ibid.

113. Church History Committee 2006, "Partial History of the Andrews Memorial Seventh-day Adventist Church," 1.

114. E. J. Heisler, "Farewell and Welcome," *West Indies Union Visitor* 19, no. 1 (1962): 5, https://1ref.us/wq (accessed January 6, 2020).

115. Alton B. Marshalleck (former business manager, Andrews Memorial Hospital) in discussion with Heather F. Fletcher, July 24, 2016.

116. Heisler, "Farewell and Welcome," 5.

117. E. J. Heisler, "Hospital Day at Andrews Memorial Hospital," *British West Indies Union Visitor* 13, no. 7, 8, & 9 (1956): 1, 2, https://1ref.us/vi (accessed January 6, 2020).

118. R. S. Blackburn, "Dr. William J. Gardner Arrives at Andrews," *British West Indies Union Visitor* 14, no. 5, 6 (1957): 2, https://1ref.us/vj (accessed January 6, 2020).

119. E. J. Heisler, "Andrews Memorial Hospital," *West Indies Union Visitor* 16, no. 2 (1959): 5, https://1ref.us/wr (accessed January 6, 2020).

120. *1959 Yearbook of the Seventh-day Adventist Denomination* (Washington, D.C.: Review and Herald Publishing Association, 1959), 271, data reported for 1958, https://1ref.us/ws (accessed January 6, 2020).

121. Heisler, "Andrews Memorial Hospital," 5.

122. Shirley Spain Gallimore (former matron, Andrews Memorial Hospital) in discussion with Karen J. Radke, July 27, 2016.

123. Heisler, "Andrews Memorial Hospital," 5.

124. *1960 Yearbook of the Seventh-day Adventist Denomination* (Washington, D.C.: Review and Herald Publishing Association, 1960), 280, data reported for 1959, https://1ref.us/wt (accessed January 6, 2020).

125. Heisler, "Andrews Memorial Hospital," 5.

126. M. G. Nembhard, ed., "We Take This Opportunity of Saying Goodbye...," *West Indies Union Visitor* 18, no. 4 (1961): 1, refer to photograph caption, https://1ref.us/wu (accessed January 6, 2020).

127. Shirley Spain Gallimore (former matron, Andrews Memorial Hospital) in discussion with Karen J. Radke, July 27, 2016.

128. General Conference of Seventh-day Adventists Executive Committee, December 6, 1956, [Minutes], s.vv. "B. G. Arellano—Bella Vista Hospital:" 780, https://1ref.us/wv (accessed January 6, 2020).

129. M. G. Nembhard, ed., "Succeeding Dr. McLaren as Medical Director...," *West Indies Union Visitor* 18, no. 4 (1961): 1, refer to photograph caption, https://1ref.us/wu (accessed January 6, 2020).

130. Rose Henry Morgan (daughter of Matron Mildred Richards Henry, Andrews Memorial Hospital) in e-mail message to Karen J. Radke, February 13, 2015.

131. E. J. Heisler, "Acting Matron for Andrews Memorial Hospital," *West Indies Union Visitor*, 19, no. 2 (1962): 3, https://1ref.us/ww (accessed January 6, 2020).

132. *1963 Yearbook of the Seventh-day Adventist Denomination* (Washington D.C.: Review and Herald Publishing Association, 1963): 328, data reported for 1962, https://1ref.us/wx (accessed January 6, 2020).

133. Ibid.

134. Alton B. Marshalleck (former business manager, Andrews Memorial Hospital) in discussion with Heather F. Fletcher, July 24, 2016.

135. *1963 Yearbook of the Seventh-day Adventist Denomination*, 328.

136. Church History Committee 2006, "Partial History of the Andrews Memorial Seventh-day Adventist Church," 1.

137. Alton B. Marshalleck (former business manager, Andrews Memorial Hospital) in discussion with Karen J. Radke, June 12, 2016.

138. Rose Henry Morgan (daughter of Matron Mildred Richards Henry, Andrews Memorial Hospital) in e-mail message to Karen J. Radke, June 30, 2016.

139. *Seventh-day Adventist Yearbook 1967* (Washington, D.C.: Review and Herald Publishing Association, 1967): 356, data reported for 1966, https://1ref.us/wy (accessed January 6, 2020).

140. *Seventh-day Adventist Yearbook 1969* (Washington D.C.: Review and Herald Publishing Association, 1969): 374, data reported for 1968, https://1ref.us/tm (accessed January 6, 2020).

141. Rose Henry Morgan (daughter of Matron Mildred Richards Henry, Andrews Memorial Hospital) in e-mail message to Karen J. Radke, June 30, 2016.

142. General Conference of Seventh-day Adventists Executive Committee, May 12, 1966, [Minutes], s.vv. "Mark Fowler, M. D.—Andrews Memorial Hospital, Jamaica:," 1494, https://1ref.us/wz (accessed January 6, 2020).

143. *Seventh-day Adventist Yearbook 1969*, 374, data reported for 1968.

144. Ibid.

145. General Conference of Seventh-day Adventists Executive Committee, April 8, 1965, [Minutes], s.vv. "Roy L. Henrickson—Jamaica:" 999, https://1ref.us/x0 (accessed January 6, 2020).

146. *Seventh-day Adventist Yearbook 1969*, 374, data reported for 1968.

147. Alton B. Marshalleck (former business manager, Andrews Memorial Hospital) in discussion with Heather F. Fletcher, July 24, 2016.

148. *Seventh-day Adventist Yearbook 1969*, 374, data reported for 1968.

149. "History of Andrews Memorial Hospital," 3. Unpublished document provided by Alton B. Marshalleck (former business manager, Andrews Memorial Hospital) to Heather F. Fletcher, July 24, 2014.

150. Jewel Henrickson, "The Fair with a Difference," *Inter-American Division Messenger* 46, no. 4 (1969): 6, 7, https://1ref.us/x1 (accessed January 6, 2020).

151. Alton B. Marshalleck (former business manager, Andrews Memorial Hospital) in discussion with Heather F. Fletcher, July 21, 2016.

152. Ibid.

153. General Conference of Seventh-day Adventists Executive Committee, August 1, 1968, [Minutes], s.vv. "Rebecca Gucilatar—Andrews Memorial Hospital:," 68-1053, https://1ref.us/x2 (accessed January 6, 2020).

154. Benjamin Baker, PhD, (assistant archivist, Office of Archives, Statistics and

Research, General Conference of Seventh-day Adventists) in e-mail message to Karen J. Radke, August 7, 2014.

155. M. Ellsworth Olsen, *A History of the Origin and Progress of Seventh-day Adventists*, Second Edition (Washington D.C.: Review and Herald Publishing Association, 1926), 269, 270.

CHAPTER FOUR

1. Benjamin Baker, PhD (assistant archivist, Office of Archives, Statistics, and Research, General Conference of Seventh-day Adventists) in e-mail message to Karen J. Radke, August 7, 2014.

2. Rebecca Gucilatar-Jakobsen, "West Indies Department of Nursing Historical Beginning," (final report submitted to West Indies College, Andrews Memorial Hospital, West Indies Union Conference, Inter-American Division of Seventh-day Adventists Department of Education, General Conference of Seventh-day Adventists Department of Education and Department of Health, 1976), 24. Heather F. Fletcher obtained document that is archived in the Department of Nursing, Northern Caribbean University, Mandeville, Jamaica.

3. Karen J. Radke, *Notes on Jamaica: 1972–1973*. Unpublished document.

4. Gucilatar-Jakobsen, "West Indies Department of Nursing Historical Beginning," 24.

5. Charles Wilkens (former physician and interim medical director, Andrews Memorial Hospital) in discussion with Karen J. Radke, March 6, 2016.

6. Sylvia Powers, ed., "Dr. Basil C. Arthur...," *The Inter-American Messenger* 43, no. 8 (1966): 11, https://1ref.us/x3 (accessed January 6, 2020).

7. General Conference of Seventh-day Adventist Executive Committee, April 30, 1970, [Minutes], s.vv. Basil Arthur, M. D.—Jamaica:" 2013, https://1ref.us/x4 (accessed January 6, 2020).

8. Gucilatar-Jakobsen, "West Indies Department of Nursing Historical Beginning," 24.

9. "Former NCU (WIC) President Dies," *Northern Caribbean University News*, https://1ref.us/vo (accessed January 6, 2020).

10. Refer to Rebecca Gucilatar-Jakobsen's biography in this book.

11. Ibid.

12. Guilatar-Jakobsen, "West Indies Department of Nursing Historical Beginning," 24, 25.

13. Ibid., 37–47.

14. Ibid., 25.

15. Ibid., 25, 26.

16. Ibid., 26.

17. Ibid., 26, 27.

18. Ibid., 27, 28.

19. Alton B. Marshalleck (former business manager, Andrews Memorial Hospital) in discussion with Karen J. Radke, December 31, 2017.

20. Gucilatar-Jakobsen, "West Indies Department of Nursing Historical Beginning," 27.

21. Ibid.

22. Ibid., 28.

23. "The Nurses and Midwives Act," September 8, 1966, Section 16, Regulations, pp. 5, 20, retrieved from https://1ref.us/x5 (accessed January 6, 2020).

24. Gucilatar-Jakobsen, "West Indies Department of Nursing Historical Beginning," 28.

25. Ibid., 46, 47.

26. Alton B. Marshalleck (former business manager, Andrews Memorial Hospital) in discussion with Karen J. Radke, December 31, 2017.

CHAPTER FIVE

1. Andrew J. Robbins, "Two More Nurses Leave for Overseas Duty," *Far Eastern Division Outlook* 48, no. 2 (1962): 20.

2. Ibid.

3. R. C. Darnell, ed., "From Here and There: Libya," *Middle East Messenger* 13, no. 3 (1964): 7, https://1ref.us/x6 (accessed January 6, 2020).

4. Middle East Division Committee, January 14, 1966, [Minutes], s.vv. "Rebecca Gucilatar Permanent Return, 1314.

5. Don A. Roth, ed., "Filipino Goes to Inter-American Division," *Far Eastern Division Outlook* (1969): 14, https://1ref.us/x7 (accessed January 6, 2020).

6. Kenneth H. Wood, ed., "Answering the Call," *Review and Herald* 146, no. 19 (1969): 24, https://1ref.us/x8 (accessed January 6, 2020).

7. General Conference of Seventh-day Adventists Executive Committee, August 1, 1968, [Minutes], s.vv. "Rebecca Gucilatar—Andrews Memorial Hospital:" 68-1053, https://1ref.us/x2 (accessed January 6, 2020).

8. Rebecca Gucilatar-Jakobsen, "West Indies Department of Nursing Historical Beginning," (final report submitted to West Indies College, Andrews Memorial Hospital, West Indies Union Conference, Inter-American Division of Seventh-day Adventists Department of Education, General Conference of Seventh-day Adventists Department of Education and Department of Health, 1976), 24. Heather F. Fletcher obtained document that is archived in the Department of Nursing, Northern Caribbean University, Mandeville, Jamaica.

9. Roth, "Filipino Goes to Inter-American Division," 14.

10. D. A. Roth, "Brief News: Far Eastern Division," *Review and Herald* 146, no. 21 (1969): 17, https://1ref.us/x9 (accessed January 6, 2020).

11. General Conference of Seventh-day Adventists Executive Committee, June 10, 1971, [Minutes], s.vv. "Rebecca Gucilitar—Furlough and Leave of Absence:," 71-524, https://1ref.us/xa (accessed January 6, 2020).

12. General Conference of Seventh-day Adventists Executive Committee, April 13, 1972, [Minutes], s.vv. "Rebecca Gucilitar—Study-Leave Extension:" 72-940, https://1ref.us/xb (accessed January 6, 2020).

13. Radke, *Notes on Jamaica: 1972–1973.*

14. Kresten Jakobsen in discussion with Karen J. Radke, September 14, 2014.

15. R. H. Gucilatar, "When You Become a Nurse," *Andrews Memorial Hospital School of Assistant Nursing Bulletin* (Kingston, Jamaica, 1969): 3, unpublished document provided by Alton B. Marshalleck (former business manager, Andrews Memorial Hospital) to Heather F. Fletcher, July 24, 2014.

16. Rebecca Gucilatar-Jakobsen, "A Crown of Glory," *College Voice* 74, no. 1 (1997): 22, copy provided by Kresten Jakobsen to Karen J. Radke, September 22, 2014.

17. Graduates (Classes of 1974, 1975, and 1976, in part) in e-mail messages to Karen J. Radke, September 2014–March 2018.

18. Kresten Jakobsen in discussion with Karen J. Radke, February 18, 2015.

CHAPTER SIX

1. Rayon Daley, "Annals of NCU 2," December 31, 2015, https://1ref.us/xc (accessed January 6, 2020).

2. M. G. Nembhard, "West Indies News Notes," *Inter-American Messenger* 47, no. 7 (1970): 11, https://1ref.us/xd (accessed January 6, 2020).

3. Daley, "Annals of NCU 2," December 31, 2015.

4. Karen J. Radke, *Notes on Jamaica: 1972–1973.* Unpublished document.

5. Ashlee Chism, MSI (assistant archivist, Office of Archives, Statistics, and Research, General Conference of Seventh-day Adventists) in e-mail message to Karen J. Radke, January 2, 2018.

6. *Seventh-day Adventist Yearbook 1973–74* (Washington, D.C.: Review and Herald Publishing Association, 1973), 367, data reported for 1972, https://1ref.us/xe (accessed January 6, 2020).

7. C. A. Holness, "West Indies Union," *Inter-American News Flashes* no. 207 (1978): 2.

8. Graduates (Class of 1974) in e-mail messages to Karen J. Radke, December 5 & 6, 2017.

9. Ibid.

10. Rebecca Gucilatar-Jakobsen, "West Indies Department of Nursing Historical Beginning," (final report submitted to West Indies College, Andrews Memorial Hospital, West Indies Union Conference, Inter-American Division of Seventh-

day Adventists Department of Education, General Conference of Seventh-day Adventists Department of Education and Department of Health, 1976), 28. Heather F. Fletcher obtained document that is archived in the Department of Nursing, Northern Caribbean University, Mandeville, Jamaica.

11. Jennifer Bartley (coordinator of academic records, Northern Caribbean University) verified coursework in e-mail message to Heather F. Fletcher, February 1, 2018.

12. Information quoted from letter addressed to Dr. H. L. Douce, WIC Academic Dean, by Julie Symes, registrar, Nursing Council of Jamaica on December 18, 1981. Heather F. Fletcher obtained document that is archived in the Department of Nursing, Northern Caribbean University, Mandeville, Jamaica.

13. Gucilatar-Jakobsen, "West Indies Department of Nursing Historical Beginning," 28.

14. "Nursing Council of Jamaica Annual Report 1971–1972, quoted in Hermie Hyacinth Hewitt, *Trailblazers in Nursing Education: A Caribbean Perspective, 1940--1986* (Kingston, Jamaica: Canoe Press, University of the West Indies, Mona, 2002), 206.

15. E. Norma Woodham, director of Nursing Education, and Enid D. Lawrence, former director of Nursing Education at University Hospital of the West Indies, "A Tribute to Greatness: Development of the Nursing Programme at NCU." Heather F. Fletcher obtained document that is archived in the Department of Nursing, Northern Caribbean University, Mandeville, Jamaica.

16. Ibid.

17. Radke, *Notes on Jamaica: 1972–1973*.

18. "Department of Nursing," *Bulletin: West Indies College, 1971– 72* (Mandeville, Jamaica: West Indies College Press, 1971), 76–83. Document obtained by Heather F. Fletcher, June 24, 2015.

19. General Conference of Seventh-day Adventists Executive Committee, June 10, 1971, [Minutes], s.vv. "Rebecca Gucilitar—Furlough and Leave of Absence:" 71-524, https://1ref.us/xa (accessed January 6, 2020).

20. Gucilatar-Jakobsen, "West Indies Department of Nursing Historical Beginning," 26.

21. Duane S. Johnson (associate secretary, General Conference of Seventh-day Adventists) in a letter to Karen J. Radke, January 15, 1970.

22. General Conference of Seventh-day Adventists Executive Committee, June 10, 1971, [Minutes], s.vv. "Rebecca Gucilitar—Furlough and Leave of Absence:" 71-524, https://1ref.us/xa (accessed January 6, 2020).

23. General Conference of Seventh-day Adventists Executive Committee, April 13, 1972, [Minutes], s.vv. "Rebecca Gucilitar—Study-Leave Extension:," 72-940, https://1ref.us/xb (accessed January 6, 2020).

24. Radke, *Notes on Jamaica: 1972–1973*.

CHAPTER SEVEN

1. Cheryl Standish (wife of Colin Standish) interviewed by Karen J. Radke, July 25, 2018.

2. Legacy Australia homepage. https://1ref.us/xf (accessed January 6, 2020).

CHAPTER EIGHT

1. Yvette A. Holness (daughter of Dr. Holness) in e-mail message to Karen J. Radke on October 10, 2017.

2. Vivian Geow (academic records office specialist, Pacific Union College, California) in discussion with Karen J. Radke, November 14, 2017.

3. Yvette A. Holness (daughter of Dr. Holness) in e-mail message to Karen J. Radke, October 11, 2017.

4. Ibid.

5. Vivian Geow (academic records office specialist, Pacific Union College, California) in discussion with Karen J. Radke, November 14, 2017.

6. Vivian Geow (academic records office specialist) and Marlo J. Waters (registrar), Pacific Union College, California, in e-mail messages to Karen J. Radke, November 16 & 17, 2017.

7. Ath Tuot (records, Alumni Association, Loma Linda University School of Medicine, California) in discussion with Karen J. Radke, November 16, 2017.

8. Yvette A. Holness (daughter of Dr. Holness) in e-mail message to Karen J. Radke, October 11, 2017.

9. Leticia Russell (Pacific Union College Alumni Office) in e-mail message to Karen J. Radke, November 13, 2017.

10. Yvette A. Holness (daughter of Dr. Holness) in discussion with Karen J. Radke, August 27, 2017, and in e-mail messages to Karen J. Radke, October 10 & 16, 2017.

11. Yvette A. Holness (daughter of Dr. Holness) in discussion with Karen J. Radke, August 27, 2017, and in e-mail message to Karen J. Radke, December 9, 2017.

12. Ashlee Chism, MSI (assistant archivist, Office of Archives, Statistics, and Research, General Conference of Seventh-day Adventists) in e-mail message to Karen J. Radke, November 18, 2015.

13. Ashlee Chism, MSI (assistant archivist, Office of Archives, Statistics, and Research, General Conference of Seventh-day Adventists) in e-mail message to Karen J. Radke, January 2, 2018.

14. *Seventh-day Adventist Yearbook 1973–74* (Washington, D.C.: Review and Herald Publishing Association, 1973), 367, data reported for 1972, https://1ref.us/xe (accessed January 6, 2020).

15. C. A. Holness, "West Indies Union," *Inter-American News Flashes* no. 207 (1978): 2.

16. Yvette A. Holness (daughter of Dr. Holness) in discussion with Karen J. Radke, August 27, 2017.

17. Yvette A. Holness (daughter of Dr. Holness) in discussion with Karen J. Radke, August 27, 2017, and in e-mail messages to Karen J. Radke, October 11, 2017, & December 9, 2017.

18. Information on a plaque that hangs beside the portrait photograph of Dr. Herbert A. Holness.

19. Yvette A. Holness (daughter of Dr. Holness) in discussion with Karen J. Radke, August 27, 2017.

CHAPTER NINE

1. General Conference of Seventh-day Adventists Executive Committee, July 29, 1971, [Minutes], s.v. "Elder and Mrs. Reinhold Klingbeil—Andrews Memorial Hospital:," 71-563, https://1ref.us/xg (accessed January 6, 2020).

2. Ashlee Chism, MSI, (assistant archivist, Office of Archives, Statistics, and Research, General Conference of Seventh-day Adventists) in e-mail message to Karen J. Radke, August 23, 2017.

3. Ashlee Chism, MSI, (assistant archivist, Office of Archives, Statistics, and Research, General Conference of Seventh-day Adventists) in e-mail message to Karen J. Radke, October 5, 2017.

4. *Seventh-day Adventist Yearbook 1971* (Washington D.C.: Review and Herald Publishing Association, 1971): 406, data reported for 1970, https://1ref.us/ux (accessed January 6, 2020).

5. Ashlee Chism, MSI, (assistant archivist, Office of Archives, Statistics, and Research, General Conference of Seventh-day Adventists) in e-mail message to Karen J. Radke, August 23, 2017.

6. Rebecca Gucilatar-Jakobsen, "West Indies Department of Nursing Historical Beginning," (final report submitted to West Indies College, Andrews Memorial Hospital, West Indies Union Conference, Inter-American Division of Seventh-day Adventists Department of Education, General Conference of Seventh-day Adventists Department of Education and Department of Health, 1976), 28. Heather F. Fletcher obtained document that is archived in the Department of Nursing, Northern Caribbean University, Mandeville, Jamaica.

7. Karen J. Radke, *Notes on Jamaica: 1972–1973*. Unpublished document.

8. Graduates from the Class of 1974 in e-mail messages to Karen J. Radke, December 6 & 8, 2017.

9. Radke, *Notes on Jamaica: 1972–1973*.

10. Leonarda Dowdie-McKenzie (Class of 1974) in e-mail message to Karen J. Radke, August 16, 2017.

11. Leonarda Dowdie-McKenzie (Class of 1974) in e-mail message to Karen J. Radke, and Sonia Kennedy-Brown (Class of 1974) in discussion with Karen J. Radke, January 11, 2018.

12. Jennifer Bartley (coordinator of academic records, Northern Caribbean University) verified coursework in e-mail message to Heather F. Fletcher, February 1, 2018.

13. Shirlene McLean-Henriques and Sonia Kennedy-Brown (Class of 1974 graduates) in e-mail messages to Karen J. Radke, September 25, 2014, and September 28, 2014, respectively.

14. Shirlene McLean-Henriques (Class of 1974) in e-mail message to Karen J. Radke, September 25, 2014.

15. Leonarda Dowdie-McKenzie (Class of 1974) in e-mail message to Karen J. Radke, September 15, 2014.

16. Radke, *Notes on Jamaica: 1972–1973*.

17. General Conference of Seventh-day Adventists Executive Committee, July 29, 1971, [Minutes], s.v. "Elder and Mrs. Reinhold Klingbeil—Andrews Memorial Hospital:," 71-563, https://1ref.us/xg (accessed January 6, 2020).

18. Leonarda Dowdie-McKenzie (Class of 1974) in e-mail message to Karen J. Radke, September 15, 2014.

19. Leonarda Dowdie-McKenzie, Sonia Kennedy-Brown, Beverley McPherson, and Beverley Tai-Binger (Class of 1974 graduates) in e-mail messages to Karen J. Radke, July 30, 2015, August 2, 2015, and September 15, 2014, respectively.

20. *Seventh-day Adventist Yearbook 1972* (Washington D.C.: Review and Herald Publishing Association, 1972): 369, 370, data reported for 1971, https://1ref.us/xh (accessed January 6, 2020).

21. Karen J. Radke with the assistance of Leonarda Dowdie-McKenzie (Class of 1974) and Rose Henry Morgan (Class of 1975).

22. Karen J. Radke with the assistance of former West Indies College nursing faculty, graduates, and Andrews Memorial Hospital staff: Leonarda Dowdie-McKenzie, Dr. Ronald Hartman, JoAnn Jones, Alton B. Marshalleck, Shirlene McLean-Henriques, Myrtle Nelson Morgan, Rose Henry Morgan, and Kenneth Morris.

23. Alton B. Marshalleck (former business manager, Andrews Memorial Hospital) and Kenneth Morris (cook, Andrews Memorial Hospital) in discussion with Karen J. Radke, December 31, 2017, and January 9, 2018, respectively.

24. Alton B. Marshalleck (former business manager, Andrews Memorial Hospital) in discussion with Karen J. Radke, June 29, 2014.

25. R. A. Primero, "Ground Breaking for Nurses Dormitory," *West Indies Union Visitor*, August-September, 1971. Publication unavailable. Copy of partial document provided by Alton B. Marshalleck (former business manager, Andrews Memorial Hospital) to Heather F. Fletcher, July 24, 2014.

26. "History of the New Nurses' Residence." Copy of unpublished document provided by Alton B. Marshalleck (former business manager, Andrews Memorial Hospital) to Heather F. Fletcher, July 24, 2014.

27. Alton B. Marshalleck (former business manager, Andrews Memorial Hospital) in discussion with Karen J. Radke, November 9, 2014.

28. Karen J. Radke with the assistance of Dr. Ronald Hartman and Alton B. Marshalleck.

29. Alton B. Marshalleck (former business manager, Andrews Memorial Hospital) in discussion with Karen J. Radke, November 9, 2014.

30. *West Indies College Bulletin 1971–1972* (Mandeville, Jamaica: West Indies College Press, 1971): 32. Document obtained by Heather F. Fletcher, June 24, 2015.

31. Alton B. Marshalleck (former business manager, Andrews Memorial Hospital) in discussion with Karen J. Radke, November 9, 2014.

32. Gucilatar-Jakobsen, "West Indies Department of Nursing Historical Beginning," 28.

33. "Programme for the Ground-Breaking Ceremony of the New Andrews Memorial Hospital." Copy of document provided by Alton B. Marshalleck (former business manager, Andrews Memorial Hospital) to Heather F. Fletcher, July 24, 2014.

34. R. A. Primero, "Andrews Memorial Hospital to be Reconstructed." *West Indies Union Visitor*, August-September, 1971. Publication unavailable. Copy of partial document provided by Alton B. Marshalleck (former business manager, Andrews Memorial Hospital) to Heather F. Fletcher, July 24, 2014.

35. Alton B. Marshalleck (former business manager, Andrews Memorial Hospital) in discussion with Karen J. Radke, June 19, 2017.

36. "Capping Ceremony for the First Class of Professional Nurses of West Indies College Department of Nursing." Copy of programme cover provided by Alton B. Marshalleck (former business manager, Andrews Memorial Hospital) to Heather F. Fletcher, July 24, 2014.

37. "Six West Indies College Nurses Graduate," *Kingston Gleaner*, December 9, 1971. Newspaper clipping provided by Alton B. Marshalleck (former business manager, Andrews Memorial Hospital) to Heather F. Fletcher, July 24, 2014.

38. Beverley McPherson and Leonarda Dowdie-McKenzie (Class of 1974 graduates) in e-mail messages to Karen J. Radke, July 19, 2015, and August 17, 2015, respectively.

39. "Six West Indies College Nurses Graduate."

40. Jennifer Bartley (coordinator of academic records, Northern Caribbean University) verified coursework in e-mail message to Heather F. Fletcher, February 1, 2018.

41. Sonia Kennedy-Brown and Beverley McPherson (Class of 1974 graduates) in e-mail messages to Karen J. Radke, March 27, 2016.

42. H. S. Walters, "Dormitory," *Inter-American Messenger Flashes*, no. 41 (1972): 2, https://1ref.us/xi (accessed January 6, 2020).

43. Alton B. Marshalleck (former business manager, Andrews Memorial Hospital) in discussion with Karen J. Radke, June 29, 2014.

44. "History of the New Nurses' Residence," 2. Copy of unpublished document provided by Alton B. Marshalleck (former business manager, Andrews Memorial Hospital) to Heather F. Fletcher, July 24, 2014.

45. Leonarda Dowdie-McKenzie (Class of 1974) in e-mail message to Karen J. Radke, January 29, 2018.

46. Jennifer Bartley (coordinator of academic records, Northern Caribbean University) verified coursework in e-mail message to Heather F. Fletcher, February 1, 2018.

47. Radke, *Notes on Jamaica: 1972–1973.*

48. Enid Lawrence in letter to Antoinette Klingbeil, July 12, 1972. Heather F. Fletcher obtained document that is archived in the Department of Nursing, Northern Caribbean University, Mandeville, Jamaica.

49. Antoinette Klingbeil in letter to Dr. Basil Arthur, May 2, 1972. Document in personal file of Karen J. Radke, Office of Archives, Statistics, and Research, General Conference of Seventh-day Adventists.

CHAPTER TEN

1. David Klingbeil (son of Antoinette and Rheinhold Klingbeil) in discussion with Karen J. Radke, October 16, 2018.

2. Benjamin Baker (assistant archivist, Office of Archives, Statistics, and Research, General Conference of Seventh-day Adventists) in e-mail message to Karen J. Radke, September 25, 2014.

3. Jonathan Klingbeil and David Klingbeil (sons of Antoinette and Reinhold Klingbeil) in discussion with Karen J. Radke, October 12, 2014, and February 22, 2015, respectively.

4. Benjamin Baker (assistant archivist, Office of Archives, Statistics, and Research, General Conference of Seventh-day Adventists) in e-mail message to Karen J. Radke, September 25, 2014.

5. Jonathan Klingbeil and David Klingbeil (sons of Antoinette and Reinhold Klingbeil) in discussion with Karen J. Radke, October 12, 2014, and February 22, 2015, respectively.

6. Rilla Klingbeil (daughter-in-law of Antoinette and Reinhold Klingbeil) in discussion with Karen J. Radke, October 16, 2018.

7. Jonathan Klingbeil and David Klingbeil (sons of Antoinette and Reinhold Klingbeil) in discussion with Karen J. Radke, October 12, 2014, and February 22, 2015, respectively.

8. Benjamin Baker (assistant archivist, Office of Archives, Statistics, and Research, General Conference of Seventh-day Adventists) in e-mail message to Karen J. Radke, September 25, 2014.

9. Karen J. Radke, *Notes on Jamaica: 1972–1973*. Unpublished document.

10. Rilla Klingbeil (daughter-in-law of Antoinette and Reinhold Klingbeil) in discussion with Karen J. Radke, January 9, 2018.

11. Benjamin Baker (assistant archivist, Office of Archives, Statistics, and Research, General Conference of Seventh-day Adventists) in e-mail message to Karen J. Radke, September 25, 2014.

12. Jonathan Klingbeil and David Klingbeil (sons of Antoinette and Reinhold Klingbeil) in discussion with Karen J. Radke, October 12, 2014, and February 22, 2015, respectively.

13. Graduates (Class of 1974) in oral and written communications with Karen J. Radke, September 2014.

14. Rilla Klingbeil (daughter-in-law of Antoinette and Reinhold Klingbeil) in discussion with Karen J. Radke, November 10, 2018.

15. Jonathan Klingbeil and David Klingbeil (sons of Antoinette and Reinhold Klingbeil) in discussion with Karen J. Radke, October 12, 2014, and February 22, 2015, respectively.

CHAPTER ELEVEN

1. Document in personal file of Karen J. Radke, Office of Archives, Statistics, and Research, General Conference of Seventh-day Adventists. File sent to Dr. Radke by Benjamin Baker, PhD, assistant archivist, August 7, 2014.

2. Karen J. Radke, *Notes on Jamaica: 1970–1973*. Unpublished document.

3. Karen J. Radke with assistance from the Class of 1975.

4. Alton B. Marshalleck (former business manager, Andrews Memorial Hospital) in discussion with Karen J. Radke, June 29, 2014.

5. Karen J. Radke with the assistance of Rose Henry Morgan (Class of 1975), October 12, 2014.

6. Karen J. Radke's letter to parents and students, September 1972. Heather F. Fletcher obtained document that is archived in the Department of Nursing, Northern Caribbean University, Mandeville, Jamaica.

7. Judith Clayton-Gomez, Leonarda Dowdie-McKenzie, Sonia Kennedy-Brown, and Shirlene McLean-Henriques (Class of 1974 graduates) in e-mail messages to Karen J. Radke, November 5, 7, & 16, 2018.

8. Joyce Malcolm (coordinator of academic records, Northern Caribbean University) in e-mail message to Heather F. Fletcher, November 6, 2015.

9. Radke, *Notes on Jamaica: 1972–1973*.

10.   Jennifer Bartley (coordinator of academic records, Northern Caribbean University) verified coursework in e-mail message to Heather F. Fletcher, February 1, 2018.

11.   Karen J. Radke with assistance from Leonarda Dowdie-McKenzie, Shirlene McLean-Henriques, and Beverley Tai-Binger (Class of 1974 graduates), March 27, 2018.

12.   Jennifer Bartley (coordinator of academic records, Northern Caribbean University) verified coursework in e-mail message to Heather F. Fletcher, February 1, 2018.

13.   Radke, *Notes on Jamaica: 1972–1973*.

14.   Ibid.

15.   "Nurses and Midwives Regulations, September 14, 1966." https://1ref.us/xj (accessed January 6, 2020).

16.   Radke, *Notes on Jamaica: 1972–1973*. Marilyn Clare-Moreau (Class of 1976) approved paragraph as written and gave permission to use her name in an e-mail message to Karen J. Radke, June 11, 2018.

17.   Radke, *Notes on Jamaica: 1972–1973*.

18.   "Department of Nursing," *BULLETIN West Indies College 1973–75* (Mandeville, Jamaica: West Indies College Press, 1973), 70.

19.   "West Indies College Department of Nursing Capping Ceremony, January 14, 1973." Copy of programme provided by Doreen Hardware (Class of 1975) in e-mail message to Karen J. Radke, September 12, 2014.

20.   Maggie Burrows-Turner (Class of 1975) in e-mail message to Karen J. Radke, May 28, 2018.

21.   "West Indies College Department of Nursing Capping Ceremony."

22.   Cheryl Standish (wife of Dr. Standish) in discussion with Karen J. Radke, July 25, 2018.

23.   Newton Hoilette, "Memorial Panorama," of the life of L. Herbert Fletcher, p. 3. According to Lee Herbert, III, L. Herbert Fletcher was more than a close friend with Dr. Newton Hoilette; he was also a father-figure to him. Programme for "Memorial Panorama and Celebration Service" provided by Dr. Ouida E. Spleen Westney.

24.   Radke, *Notes on Jamaica: 1972–1973*.

25.   Hermi Hyacinth Hewitt, *Trailblazers in Nursing Education: A Caribbean Perspective, 1946–1986* (Kingston, Jamaica: Canoe Press, University of the West Indies, Mona, 2002), 104–165.

26.   Gertrude Hildegarde Swaby (prominent leader in nursing education) in discussions with Karen J. Radke, 1972–1973.

27.   Ibid.

28.   Peace Corps, n.d., retrieved from https://1ref.us/xk (accessed January 6, 2020).

29. Peace Corps, n.d., retrieved from https://1ref.us/xl (accessed January 6, 2020).

30. Radke, *Notes on Jamaica: 1972–1973.*

31   Ibid.

32. Ibid.

33. Ibid.

34. Alton B. Marshalleck (former business manager, Andrews Memorial Hospital) and Sonia Kennedy-Brown (Class of 1974) in discussion with Karen J. Radke, November 9, 2014, and March 28, 2018, respectively.

35. Marilyn Clare-Moreau (Class of 1976) in discussion with Karen J. Radke, January 11, 2015.

36. Edna Ashmeade (faculty, WIC Department of Nursing Education) in discussion with Karen J. Radke, 2015.

37. Radke, *Notes on Jamaica: 1972–1973.* Additional assistance from the Classes of 1975 and 1976 in e-mail messages to Karen J. Radke, 2015.

38. Radke, *Notes on Jamaica: 1972–1973.* Additional assistance from Marilyn Clare-Moreau (Class of 1976) and Rose Henry Morgan (Class of 1975), 2015. Further assistance from Leonarda Dowdie-McKenzie (Class of 1974), 2019.

39. Radke, *Notes on Jamaica: 1972–1973.* Additional assistance from Evadne Cox-McCleary and Rose Henry Morgan (Class of 1975 graduates), April 6, 2018, and March 12, 2018, respectively.

40. Radke, *Notes on Jamaica: 1972–1973.* Additional assistance from Marilyn Clare-Moreau (Class of 1976) and Rose Henry Morgan (Class of 1975), 2015.

41. Radke, *Notes on Jamaica: 1972–1973.* Additional assistance from Sonia Kennedy-Brown and Shirlene McLean-Henriques (Class of 1974 graduates), November 7, 2018.

42. Radke, *Notes on Jamaica: 1972–1973.* Additional assistance from Leonarda Dowdie-McKenzie, Shirlene McLean-Henriques, and Beverley Tai-Binger (Class of 1974 graduates), March 27, 2018.

43. Radke, *Notes on Jamaica: 1972–1973.* Additional assistance from Evadne Cox-McCleary and Rose Henry Morgan (Class of 1975 graduates), April 6, 2018, and March 12, 2018, respectively.

44. Doreen Hardware (Class of 1975) in e-mail message to Karen J. Radke, March 19, 2018.

45. Radke, *Notes on Jamaica: 1972–1973.*

46. Ibid.

47. Kenneth H. Wood, ed., "To New Posts," *Advent Review and Sabbath Herald* 150, no. 30 (1973): 23, https://1ref.us/xm (accessed January 6, 2020).

48. Alton B. Marshalleck (former business manager, Andrews Memorial Hospital) in discussion with Karen J. Radke, November 9, 2014.

49. "Department of Nursing," *BULLETIN West Indies College 1973–75* (Mandeville, Jamaica: West Indies College Press, 1973), 68–70.

50. "WIC Standing Committees: 1973–1974." Copy of document provided by Alton B. Marshalleck (former business manager, Andrews Memorial Hospital) to Heather F. Fletcher, July 24, 2014. Such documents are retained in the president's office, Northern Caribbean University, Mandeville, Jamaica.

51. Radke, *Notes on Jamaica: 1972–1973.*

52. Sonia Kennedy's letter in personal files of Karen J. Radke, 2018.

CHAPTER TWELVE

1. Karen J. Radke, author, April 12, 2019.

CHAPTER THIRTEEN

1. Newton Hoilette, "Memorial Panorama," of the life of L. Herbert Fletcher, p. 2. According to Lee Herbert Fletcher, III, L. Herbert Fletcher, was more than a close friend with Dr. Newton Hoilette; he was also a father-figure to him. Programme for "Memorial Panorama and Celebration Service" provided by Dr. Ouida E. Spleen Westney.

2. Olive Fletcher verified date of birth for her husband, L. Herbert Fletcher, in discussion with Karen J. Radke, July 10, 2018. She also mentioned to Karen J. Radke on July 19, 2018, that her husband enjoyed woodworking and gave examples of the wood items he made. Olive Fletcher in conversation with Karen Radke on October 10, 2019, commented that her husband enjoyed playing the musical saw.

3. Hoilette, "Memorial Panorama," 2.

4. Ibid., 2, 3.

5. "Biography of Dr. Herbert Fletcher," https://1ref.us/zb (accessed February 4, 2020).

6. Hoilette, "Memorial Panorama," 3.

7. Ibid.

8. Ibid.

9. "Memory of Lee Herbert Fletcher (1929–2009)," https://1ref.us/zb (accessed February 4, 2020).

10. Hoilette, "Memorial Panorama," 3.

11. Ibid.

12. "Herbert Fletcher University," https://1ref.us/zb (accessed February 2, 2020).

13. Hoilette, "Memorial Panorama," 1.

CHAPTER FOURTEEN

1. Rebecca Gucilatar-Jakobsen, "West Indies Department of Nursing Historical Beginning," (final report submitted to West Indies College, Andrews Memorial

Hospital, West Indies Union Conference, Inter-American Division of Seventh-day Adventists Department of Education, General Conference of Seventh-day Adventists Department of Education and Department of Health, 1976), 32, 33. Heather F. Fletcher obtained document that is archived in the Department of Nursing, Northern Caribbean University, Mandeville, Jamaica.

2.   Ilene (Irene) Gentles-Patrick (Class of 1976) and Maggie Burrows-Turner (Class of 1975) in e-mail messages to Karen J. Radke, March 7, 2018, and March 14, 2018, respectively.

3.   Karen J. Radke, *Notes on Jamaica: 1972–1973.* Unpublished document.

4.   Gucilatar-Jakobsen, "West Indies Department of Nursing Historical Beginning," 31–33.

5.   Marilyn Clare-Moreau (Class of 1976) in discussion with Karen J. Radke, March 15, 2015.

6.   Audrey Grant-Lewin (Class of 1976) in discussion with Karen J. Radke, March 20, 2018.

7.   Jennifer Bartley (coordinator of academic records, Northern Caribbean University) verified coursework in e-mail message to Heather F. Fletcher, February 1, 2018. Rose Henry Morgan (Class of 1975) in e-mail message to Karen J. Radke regarding Mona Rehabilitation Centre, March 26, 2018.

8.   Rose Henry Morgan (Class of 1975) in e-mail message to Karen J. Radke, March 13, 2018.

9.   Jennifer Bartley (coordinator of academic records, Northern Caribbean University) verified coursework in e-mail message to Heather F. Fletcher, February 1, 2018.

10. Ibid.

11. Gucilatar-Jakobsen, "West Indies Department of Nursing Historical Beginning," 36. Additional information from Leonarda Dowdie-McKenzie (Class of 1974) in e-mail message to Karen J. Radke, August 3, 2015.

12. Judith Clayton Gomez, Sonia Kennedy-Brown, and Shirlene McLean-Henriques (Class of 1974 graduates) in e-mail messages to Karen J. Radke, March 8, 2018.

13. Elaine Haughton (Class of 1976) in e-mail message to Karen J. Radke, March 31, 2018.

14. Joan Collins-Ricketts (Class of 1976) in e-mail message to Karen J. Radke, August 28, 2018.

15. Graduates (Class of 1976) in discussion with Karen J. Radke, March 4 & 20, 2018.

16. Leonarda Dowdie-McKenzie and Sonia Kennedy-Brown (Class of 1974 graduates) and Rose Henry Morgan (Class of 1975) in email messages to Karen J. Radke, April 1–2, 2018.

17. Ilene (Irene) Gentles-Patrick (Class of 1976) and Judith Clayton Gomez (Class of 1974) in communication with Karen J. Radke, March 4, 2018, and April 5, 2018, respectively.

18. Ilene (Irene) Gentles-Patrick and Audrey Grant-Lewin (Class of 1976 graduates) in discussion with Karen J. Radke, March 4, 2018, and March 20, 2018, respectively.

19. M. G. Nembhard (secretary, West Indies Union Conference) in letter to Nurse R. H. Gucilatar dated December 27, 1973. Heather F. Fletcher obtained document that is archived in the Department of Nursing, Northern Caribbean University, Mandeville, Jamaica. Additional information in Radke, *Notes on Jamaica: 1972–1973*.

20. E. Norma Woodham, director of nursing education, and Enid D. Lawrence, former director of nursing education at University Hospital of the West Indies, "A Tribute to Greatness: Development of the Nursing Programme at NCU." Date not given. Heather F. Fletcher obtained document that is archived in the Department of Nursing, Northern Caribbean University, Mandeville, Jamaica.

21. "Pinning and Dedication Programme, June 1, 1974." Copy of programme provided by Alton B. Marshalleck (former business manager, Andrews Memorial Hospital) to Heather F. Fletcher, July 24, 2014.

22. Sonia Kennedy-Brown (Class of 1974) in e-mail message to Karen J. Radke, September 30, 2018.

23. "Pinning and Dedication Programme, June 1, 1974."

24. Leonarda Dowdie-McKenzie (Class of 1974) in e-mail message to Karen J. Radke, April 30, 2018.

25. "Pinning and Dedication Programme, June 1, 1974."

26. Graduate (Class of 1974) in e-mail message to Karen J. Radke, August 17, 2016.

27. I. B. Benson, "Nursing Degrees Granted," *Inter-American Messenger Flashes*, no. 91 (1974): 1, https://1ref.us/xn (accessed January 6, 2020).

28. "West Indies College Commencement Programme 1974." Information obtained by Heather F. Fletcher on May 11, 2016.

29. "Mr. Dudley Ransford Grant." https://1ref.us/xo (accessed January 6, 2020).

30. Shirlene McLean-Henriques (Class of 1974) in e-mail message to Karen J. Radke, March 9, 2018.

31. Sonia Kennedy-Brown (Class of 1974) in discussion with Karen J. Radke, January 28, 2019.

32. Alton B. Marshalleck (former business manager, Andrews Memorial Hospital) in discussion with Karen J. Radke, November 9, 2014.

CHAPTER FIFTEEN

1. Rose Henry Morgan (daughter of Matron Mildred Henry) in e-mail message to Karen J. Radke, February 13, 2015.

2. Ibid.

3. Ibid.

4. Ibid.

5. Karen J. Radke, *Notes on Jamaica: 1972–1973.* Unpublished document.

6. Ibid.

7. Rose Henry Morgan (daughter of Matron Mildred Henry) in e-mail message to Karen J. Radke, February 13, 2015.

8. Ibid.

9. Graduates (Classes of 1974, 1975, and 1976, in part) in e-mail messages to Karen J. Radke, September 2014– March 2018.

10. The Florence Nightingale Pledge. https://1ref.us/xp (accessed January 6, 2020).

11. Graduate (Class of 1974) in e-mail message to Karen J. Radke, September 15, 2014.

12. Rose Henry Morgan (daughter of Matron Mildred Henry) in e-mail messages to Karen J. Radke, February 13, 2015 and October 6, 2019.

CHAPTER SIXTEEN

1. Rose Henry Morgan and Maxine Smith-Webley (Class of 1975 graduates) in communications with Karen J. Radke, March 12, 2018, and March 13, 2018, respectively.

2. Joan Collins-Ricketts (Class of 1976) in discussion with Karen J. Radke, September 13, 2018.

3. Rose Henry Morgan (Class of 1975) in e-mail message to Karen J. Radke, August 18, 2014.

4. Leonarda Dowdie-McKenzie (Class of 1974) and Audrey Grant-Lewin (Class of 1976) in communications with Karen J. Radke, January 30, 2018, and March 20, 2018, respectively.

5. Marilyn Clare-Moreau (Class of 1976) in discussion with Karen J. Radke, March 15, 2015.

6. Rebecca Gucilatar-Jakobsen, "West Indies Department of Nursing Historical Beginning," (final report submitted to West Indies College, Andrews Memorial Hospital, West Indies Union Conference, Inter-American Division of Seventh-day Adventists Department of Education, General Conference of Seventh-day Adventists Department of Education and Department of Health, 1976), 33. Heather F. Fletcher obtained document that is archived in the Department of Nursing, Northern Caribbean University, Mandeville, Jamaica.

7. Alton B. Marshalleck (former business manager, Andrews Memorial Hospital) in discussion with Karen J. Radke, November 9, 2014.

8. Judith Clayton Gomez and Leonarda Dowdie-McKenzie (Class of 1974 graduates) and Rose Henry Morgan (Class of 1975) in e-mail messages to Karen J. Radke, September 11, 2014, January 11, 2018, and September 10, 2018, respectively.

9. Mazie A. Herin, (associate secretary, Nursing Education and Nursing Service, Medical Department, General Conference of Seventh-day Adventists), "West

Indies College Department of Nursing and Andrews Memorial Hospital Department of Nursing Service," (unpublished document, Box 2, Folder 2, Muriel E. Chapman Collection: The History of Seventh-day Adventist Nursing [collection 270], Center for Adventist Research, James White Library, Andrews University, Berrien Springs, Michigan), 20. Consultation visit in September 1974. Document sent by Tamara Karr, administrative assistant, Center for Adventist Research, in e-mail message to Karen J. Radke, November 13, 2015. Used with permission of Jim Ford, associate director, May 24, 2017.

10. Gucilatar-Jakobsen, "West Indies Department of Nursing Historical Beginning," 29.

11. Radke, *Notes on Jamaica: 1972–1973*.

12. Alton B. Marshalleck (former business manager, Andrews Memorial Hospital) in discussion with Karen J. Radke, September 23, 2018.

13. Ruth M. White, Dr. PH, RN, "Visit to West Indies College and Andrews Memorial Hospital, January 15–20, 1978," Report No. 1, pp. 1, 4. Heather F. Fletcher obtained document that is archived in the Department of Nursing, Northern Caribbean University, Mandeville, Jamaica.

14. Rose Henry Morgan (Class of 1975) in e-mail message to Karen J. Radke, August 13, 2014.

15. Rebecca H. Gucilatar sent letter with enclosed copies of contract to Enid Lawrence, February 11, 1975. Heather F. Fletcher obtained document that is archived in the Department of Nursing, Northern Caribbean University, Mandeville, Jamaica.

16. Gucilatar-Jakobsen, "West Indies Department of Nursing Historical Beginning," 35.

17. Kresten Jakobsen (husband of Rebecca Gucilatar-Jakobsen) in discussion with Karen J. Radke, September 14, 2014.

18. "Pinning and Dedication Programme, May 31, 1975." Copy of document provided by Doreen Hardware (Class of 1975) in e-mail message to Karen J. Radke, September 12, 2014.

19. Evadne Cox-McCleary (Class of 1975) provided title of song in e-mail message to Karen J. Radke, May 27, 2018.

20. "West Indies College Fifty-third Annual Graduation, May Thirty to June One, Nineteen Hundred and Seventy-five." Copy of programme provided by Doreen Hardware (Class of 1975) in e-mail message to Karen J. Radke, September 12, 2014.

21. M. Dawn Ottley-Nelson-Barnes, "Esther Harriott Ottley." https://1ref.us/xq (accessed January 6, 2020).

22. Maggie Burrows-Turner, Rose Henry Morgan, and Maxine Smith-Webley (Class of 1975 graduates) in e-mail messages to Karen J. Radke, March 12–14, 2018.

CHAPTER SEVENTEEN

1. Alton B. Marshalleck provided information in a written communication to Heather F. Fletcher, July 21, 2016, and in discussion with Karen J. Radke, June 19, 2017.

CHAPTER EIGHTEEN

1. Rebecca Gucilatar-Jakobsen, "West Indies Department of Nursing Historical Beginning," (final report submitted to West Indies College, Andrews Memorial Hospital, West Indies Union Conference, Inter-American Division of Seventh-day Adventists Department of Education, General Conference of Seventh-day Adventists Department of Education and Department of Health, 1976), 33, 34. Heather F. Fletcher obtained document that is archived in the Department of Nursing, Northern Caribbean University, Mandeville, Jamaica.

2. Capping and Candlelighting Ceremony for the Fifth Class of West Indies College Department of Nursing, November 16, 1975. Heather F. Fletcher obtained document that is archived in the Department of Nursing, Northern Caribbean University, Mandeville, Jamaica.

3. Gucilatar-Jakobsen, "West Indies Department of Nursing Historical Beginning," 30.

4. Ibid.

5. H. S. Walters in letter to Mrs. R. Gucilatar-Jakobsen, April 21, 1976. Heather F. Fletcher obtained document that is archived in the Department of Nursing, Northern Caribbean University, Mandeville, Jamaica.

6. Gucilatar-Jakobsen, "West Indies Department of Nursing Historical Beginning," 35, 36.

7. Ibid., 36.

8. Ibid., 34, 35.

9. Karen J. Radke, *Notes on Jamaica: 1972–1973*.

10. Gucilatar-Jakobsen, "West Indies Department of Nursing Historical Beginning," 35.

11. "Nursing," *West Indies College Bulletin: 1976–1978*, (Mandeville, Jamaica: West Indies College Press, 1976), 95–99.

12. Gucilatar-Jakobsen, "West Indies Department of Nursing Historical Beginning," 46, 47.

13. Audrey Grant-Lewin (Class of 1976) in discussion with Karen J. Radke, March 20, 2018.

14. Gucilatar-Jakobsen, "West Indies Department of Nursing Historical Beginning," 31.

15. Marilyn Clare-Moreau (Class of 1976) in discussion with Karen J. Radke, March 15, 2015.

16. "Pinning and Dedication Programme, June 5, 1976." Heather F. Fletcher obtained document that is archived in the Department of Nursing, Northern Caribbean University, Mandeville, Jamaica.

17. "West Indies College Fifty-Fourth Commencement Programme." Heather F. Fletcher obtained document that is archived in the Department of Nursing, Northern Caribbean University, Mandeville, Jamaica.

18. Marilyn Clare-Moreau (Class of 1976) in discussion with Karen J. Radke, March 15, 2015.

19. Audrey Grant-Lewin (Class of 1976) in e-mail message to Karen J. Radke, March 26, 2018.

20. Audrey Grant-Lewin (Class of 1976) in discussion with Karen J. Radke, March 20, 2018.

21. Audrey Grant-Lewin (Class of 1976) in e-mail message to Karen J. Radke, March 26, 2018.

22. Gucilatar-Jakobsen, "West Indies Department of Nursing Historical Beginning," 30.

CHAPTER NINETEEN

1. Karen J. Radke, acting chairman from 1972 to 1973, Department of Nursing Education, West Indies College (now Northern Caribbean University).

CHAPTER TWENTY

1. Heather F. Fletcher, director, Department of Nursing, Northern Caribbean University, February 21, 2019.

2. Ibid.

3. "Department of Nursing," *Undergraduate Bulletin 2018–2020* (Mandeville, Jamaica: Northern Caribbean University Press, 2018), 522.

4. Ibid., 526, 527.

5. Fletcher, director, Department of Nursing.

6. Ibid.

7. "Department of Nursing," *Undergraduate Bulletin*, 522.

8. Fletcher, director, Department of Nursing.

9. *American Heart Association Guidelines for Cardiopulmonary Resuscitation and Emergency Cardiovascular Care, 2015*, with annual updates, https://1ref.us/xr (accessed January 6, 2020).

10. Fletcher, director, Department of Nursing.

11. "Department of Nursing," *Undergraduate Bulletin*, 521.

12. Fletcher, director, Department of Nursing.

Appendix

Faculty

West Indies College Baccalaureate Nursing Programme
Andrews Memorial Hospital Campus

Milton Anderson

Gretel Ashley, BSc, RN

Edna Ashmeade, RN

Roy Ashmeade, MDiv

Lucille Bennett, RN, CM

James Boyd

C. Brooks, RN, CM

M. Carr, RN, CM

Marilyn Clare, BSc, RN

Judith Clayton, BSc, RN

Hermina Douglas, BSc, RN, CM

Leonarda Dowdie-McKenzie, BSc, RN

Mabel Dwyer-Kerr, RN, CM

Beryl Ellis, RN, CM

L. Jean Fletcher, RN, CM

Moira Gallant, MPH, RN, CM

Shirley Gallimore, BSc, RN

Beryl Gilpin, RN, CM

Rebecca Gucilatar-Jakobsen, MSc, RN

Glee Hartman, BSc, RN

Ronald Hartman, MD

Mildred Henry, BSc, RN, CM

Sonia Henry, RN, CM

David D. Higgins, MPH

Isidore B. Hodge, BTh

Anna Hoehn, BA, RN

Edward Hoehn, MD

Herbert Holness, MD

Marcheta Holness, MA

M. Hutchinson, RN, CM

Catherine Jamieson, RN, CM

Janet Jones, RN

JoAnn Jones, BSc, RN

Antoinette Klingbeil, MSc, RN

Reinhold Klingbeil, MPH, MSc, MA

Norve Manalo, RN

Alton B. Marshalleck, BSc

A. Muschett, RN

Rosella Nesbitt

T. Palima, BSc, RN, CM

Y. Parker, EAN

Lillymae Patrickson

Paterno Q. Primero, MD

Shirley Purchas, RN

Karen J. Radke, MSc, RN

Mrs. Robinson

Erma L. Serles, RN

Hyacinth Smith, RN

Jerome Stern, MD

H. A. Taffe, BTh

Larry Versio

C. Wilson, RN, CM

Lorna Wynter, RN

Karen J. Radke with the assistance of Heather F. Fletcher and graduates from the Classes of 1974, 1975, and 1976. Faculty are those who taught courses, gave lectures, and/or were clinical preceptors at various times from September 1, 1971, to August 31, 1976. The authors apologize for lack of information regarding some credentials and to anyone whose name was inadvertently omitted from the list.

Reviews

"Dr. Karen Radke and Dr. Heather Fletcher have in their book, *A Vision Becomes Reality*," outlined the beginnings of the baccalaureate nursing programme at West Indies College, Jamaica, in 1970. They have given a historical and insightful look at the forethought and vision of Hiram S. Walters, then Chairman of the West Indies College Board, to encourage the development of the baccalaureate degree nursing programme into the college curriculum.

"These authors take us on a journey that shows the faith and courage of visionary administrators, teachers, relevant persons, and organizations within the Seventh-day Adventist church school system and government institutions, as they provided expertise and direction. Students under their tutelage honed their skills to serve the region and the world as evidenced by the early graduates, who set the stage for those who would follow their pioneering footsteps.

"A must read for those who seek information on nursing in the Caribbean region of comparable world standard. The informative tone is clear and allows for easy reading. The book has also well-documented historical information that displays the integrity of its work. *A Vision Becomes Reality*" is a fitting testament as the Nursing Department of West Indies College (now Northern Caribbean University) celebrates its fiftieth anniversary in 2020."

— *Beverly Henry, JP, MA*
Chairman, Nursing Education Advisory Committee
Former Assistant Vice-President, Student Services and Records
Northern Caribbean University, Jamaica

"This book is an example of what I wish could be written about the history of every Adventist nursing program. It is a story of visionary leadership on the part of church leaders who believed that the highest level of nursing education and practice was worth striving for in Adventist institutions. It is also a story of commitment and self-sacrificing hard work by missionary and national nurses who developed the first BSc in nursing program in Jamaica. By documenting their challenges and success, Radke and Fletcher provide a valuable contribution to archiving the legacy of Adventist nursing education globally which can be described as courageous, innovative, and ahead of national norms."

— *Patricia S. Jones, PhD, RN, FAAN*
Distinguished Emerita Professor
Loma Linda University School of Nursing, California, USA
Associate Director, Department of Health Ministries
General Conference of Seventh-day Adventists, Silver Spring, Maryland, USA

"The authors of this book have provided a rich history of the first baccalaureate nursing program in Jamaica enriched with much personal detail to the extent that I, a person of no medical background, found the story fascinating. From the moment of dynamic young Hiram Walter's dream of a baccalaureate nursing program being offered on the campuses of West Indies College (now Northern Caribbean University) and Andrews Memorial Hospital until the first graduating class marched down the aisle, my heart was warmed with the patient, unfaltering tenacity of those who shared his dream. It was rewarding to read of their strong faith and to watch a program of such small beginnings flourish, though not without struggles, under God's protecting hand. The book closes with comments from former students sharing their memories and, best of all, for this reader, a collection of their achievements as they moved out into the world to bless others with their healing skills. What a contribution they have made, not only in Jamaica, but beyond."

— *June Kimball Strong*
Prolific Author and Speaker
Upstate New York, USA

About the Authors

Karen J. Radke, PhD, RN
Photo: Courtesy of the University of Rochester Medical Center, New York.

Karen J. Radke is a nurse, physiologist, educator, researcher, author, and administrator. She was acting chairman, West Indies College Department of Nursing Education, (now Northern Caribbean University Department of Nursing) in Jamaica from 1972 to1973. Her degrees in nursing are from Loma Linda University in California (BSc), Boston University in Massachusetts (MSc), and Texas Woman's University (MSc-Family Nurse Clinician). After working as a public health nurse and family nurse practitioner, Radke earned a PhD in physiology with a minor in pharmacology from Indiana University School of Medicine and then did a two-year postdoctoral research fellowship in the Department of Physiology, College of Medicine, University of Tennessee Health Science Center, Memphis. Radke taught at various colleges and universities in schools of nursing and medicine for twenty-five years. Besides teaching, Radke conducted research on hormones that influence renal function and blood pressure at the University of Rochester, New York. She presented her work at national and international scientific conferences and has many publications in scholarly journals. Later, Radke was associate dean for academic affairs, director of graduate studies, and professor, University at Buffalo School of Nursing, The State University of New York. She has garnered several honours and awards. Dr. Radke is retired.

Heather Faith Fletcher, PhD, RN
Photo: Courtesy of Northern Caribbean University.

Heather Faith Fletcher was director of the Department of Nursing at Northern Caribbean University, Jamaica, from 2014 to 2019. Previously, she was director from 2001 to 2008 after serving as acting director for two years. She taught for more than twenty-six years at Northern Caribbean University. Fletcher is a graduate of West Indies College (now Northern Caribbean University) with a bachelor of science degree in nursing and is a registered nurse. She is also a graduate of Loma Linda University, having earned a master of science degree in nursing with focuses on gerontology and on nursing education as well as a PhD in nursing with emphasis on geriatric health promotion. Dr. Fletcher's research is on caregiver burden, health literacy, and self-care in older adults. For the last twenty years she has given many national and international presentations on geriatric issues. Furthermore, she has published articles in academic and professional journals, magazines, and *The Gleaner,* a major Jamaican newspaper. Fletcher is the recipient of several accolades. To name a few, she was inducted into The Honor Society of Nursing, Sigma Theta Tau International. She has received awards for excellence in teaching and in administration from Northern Caribbean University. Fletcher provides professional services to organizations that relate to the welfare of older adults, the vulnerable, and the poor. She also contributes to nation building in her capacity as a consultant and mentor.